P9-BBP-964

SMALL
CHANGE

Susan *and* Larry Terkel

# SMALL Change

## It's the Little Things in Life That Make a Big Difference!

jeremy p. tarcher/penguin
a member of penguin group (usa) inc.
new york

Most Tarcher/Penguin books are available at special quantity discounts for bulk purchase for sales promotions, premiums, fund-raising, and educational needs. Special books or book excerpts also can be created to fit specific needs. For details, write Penguin Group (USA) Inc. Special Markets, 375 Hudson Street, New York, NY 10014.

Jeremy P. Tarcher/Penguin
a member of
Penguin Group (USA) Inc.
375 Hudson Street
New York, NY 10014
www.penguin.com


Published simultaneously in Canada

Library of Congress Cataloging-in-Publication Data

Terkel, Susan Neiburg.
Small change: it's the little things in life that make a big difference! / Susan and Larry Terkel.
p. cm.
ISBN 1-58542-359-9
1. Self-actualization (Psychology). I. Terkel, Larry, 1947–.
II. Title.
BF637 S4T46 2004 2004048084
158.1—dc22

Printed in the United States of America
10 9 8 7 6 5 4 3 2 1

*Book design by Deborah Kerner/Dancing Bears Design*

*Illustrations by Brian Garvey*

# Acknowledgments

Our deepest appreciation goes to our dear friend Lorna Greenberg, for her remarkable generosity, from first draft to final deadline. We would also like to express gratitude to our agent, Harvey Klinger, for his enthusiasm and wise counsel, and a special thank-you to our editor, Sara Carder, for embracing the concept of "small change" and displaying such stewardship toward it.

Several kind souls read over the manuscript in its various stages and gave us honest and (thankfully) constructive criticism, as well as moral support. Thank you to Pat Jenkins, Greg Cloyd, M.D., Nancy Levin, Margaret Tucker, and James Wilkens.

For inspiring so much of the wisdom and humor in the book, we thank our beloved family, especially our parents, Deborah and Sidney Neiburg and Ruth and Maury Terkel, and our children, Ari and Alicia Terkel, Marni and Jason Gardner, and Dave Terkel.

Much information had to be researched, and many facts had to be checked. For this we want to thank Alyse and Peter Blumberg, Marc Terkel, Rabbi Susan Stone, Kevin Aiken, D.D.S., Joshua Rubin, Paul Nowell, Molly White, Mitch Fromm, M.D., Deborah and Ted Furst, Ed and Joan Broadfield, Don Bak, Bob Dean, Hudson Library & Historical Society research librarians Lou Dobos, Matt Tarczy, Margie Smith, Monica Knooihuizen, and Mary Kenney and the American Automobile Association.

Sometimes we just needed to run an idea by someone. Thank you, Katie Coulton, Ann Hanna, Stephanie Stanziano, Marilyn Wise, Dean White, Jenny Marino, and Joel MacDonald.

Max Weinstein, you are our hero, for the important small change you made in your life after reading one of the chapters.

Thank you to Rick and John Hanna for letting us make Saywell's our office away from home. What a great place to read and write.

Speaking of places, we would like to acknowledge how much we have learned over the years at Omega Institute, Kripalu, the Chautauqua Institution, and the Yoga Retreat on Paradise Island.

Finally, thank you to all the other people who taught us what we wanted or needed to learn, including Naomi and Jerry Burstein, Bernice Davidson, Sue and Bert Goldberg, Annie Mae Hardaway, Joe Moran, Joshua Halberstam, Ph.D., Neil Thackaberry, George Klein, B.K.S. Iyengar, Paula Rubenstein, Sally Brashear, Kim Saporito, Susie Hughes, Rabbi David Wice, Pir Vilayat Inayat Khan, Swami Satchidananda, and Larry's students at the Spiritual Life Society. Thank you to Matt and Gennie Lerner, Joan Brandon, Rob Blaine, Carson Heiner, and Joan Van Osdol for sharing our vision there.

One piece of advice in this book is to remember to count your blessings. We feel blessed by all the people who helped us on this project, not only the ones we have just singled out but all those who have given us the spiritual richness we treasure in our lives.

# Contents

Introduction: A Better Way to a Better You *1*

1. How to Apply Small Change to Your Life *9*

2. Small Changes for Better Health *27*

3. Small Changes for Better Relationships *81*

4. Small Changes for a Healthier, More Creative Mind *129*

5. Small Change at Work *183*

6. Small Change for More Happiness *227*

Conclusion: A Little Pep Talk *276*

In memory of

Larry's beloved mother, Ruth

Klein Terkel, and

Susan's beloved uncle,

Jerome A. Burstein,

who appreciated a good workout,

a good relationship,

a good deed,

and a good joke.

# Introduction

## A Better Way to a Better You

Small change adds up. This is worth repeating: small change adds up. Empty your small change into a jar every day, and watch the total add up over time. Make small changes in your daily habits—such as your meals or snacks, your relationships, your work, or your leisure—and watch those changes gradually accumulate into a much healthier, happier, and more satisfying life.

An angle of only one degree is difficult to draw on a piece of paper. It is too small. If a flight from New York to Los Angeles is off course by just one degree, the plane will arrive closer to Tijuana, Mexico, than Los Angeles. The farther it travels, the more widely it misses its destination.

This is what happens to us in life. We drift off course.

What once seemed like a fabulous job has become tedious or frustrating. What was once a great relationship has lost its luster. The body has drifted out of shape. Like the pilot, we find ourselves off course. What are we to do?

Many advice-givers say to change direction completely. These advisers usually suggest radical changes or big makeovers. Returning to the New York–Los Angeles flight analogy, the advisers might say to change planes in Chicago. Worse, they might even suggest that the pilot return to New York and start over!

But there is good news. Small changes can get us back on course as easily as they can lead us off course. Either for you or against you, *small change adds up.*

Here is more good news. Your life is probably *not* as big a mess as you think. You are *not* bad, weak, unlovable, or out of control. People in search of self-improvement are usually just off course. Our transcontinental pilot needs to make only small adjustments along the way in order to arrive at the desired destination.

Granted, there *are* times in life when a big change is necessary. An abusive relationship or a life-threatening disease may need immediate and dramatic action. Most problems, though, have not reached the crisis stage, and for those problems, a small change approach can be the best way to go.

*Small change is powerful.* The power of small change lies in how much easier small changes are to initiate and maintain, and how meaningful are the patterns they create.

Replace a soft drink with water at just one meal—say, lunch. With this small change, you will drink approximately forty more gallons of water per year, while *not* drinking forty gallons of carbonated sugar. You will also save up to fifty thousand calories and as much as five hundred dollars.

Walk to the next bus stop instead of the closest one. In one year, you will walk more than 150 miles more than if you had not changed your routine. This is the equivalent of walking from New York to Philadelphia and back each year. In ten years you will have walked more than 1,500 miles.

Consciously say, "I love you," at the end of every phone conversation with a life partner, and it will reinforce the message for both of you, adding tens of thousands of endearments over the course of a relationship. Small change adds up!

*Small change is a gentle pathway to self-improvement.* By making small changes, one at a time, you go easy on yourself. You're not challenging yourself to become a new you overnight; you are tackling one small issue, such as taking a breath before reacting to small annoyances or doing three minutes of stretching in the morning. You give yourself positive reinforcement along the way as you succeed in making each small change. With each accomplishment you gain confidence in your ability to make changes.

*Small changes, while not always easy, are easier than big changes or massive makeovers.* We learned in high school science class that objects in motion will always follow the *path of least resistance.* We also learned the law of inertia: objects in motion tend to stay in motion, and objects at rest tend to stay at rest. Habits, especially those acquired over a long period of time, follow the same laws of nature—perhaps the reason they are so difficult to change!

Small change suggests that you honor these laws by making a *series* of small changes rather than trying to change more than you can handle. Further, if you focus on just one habit at a time, you will face less resistance than if you focus on many at once. Look at the average dieter, for example. Using small change, she or he would focus on changing one behavior before moving on to the next change. This gentle approach is clearly easier than starting a daily exercise program *and* adding four glasses of water to a daily routine *and* remembering to eat more vegetables *and* limiting high-calorie foods *and* controlling portions—all at the same time!

*Small changes are, well, small.* When Susan decided to market her painted wooden knobs, she knew that she would have to improve her painting techniques or the knobs would not be a commercial success. She asked a number of experienced artists for help. Most offered to show her how to paint a rose—the way they painted roses.

Susan's friend Paula took a different approach and started from the knobs that Susan had already painted. "We are going to improve what you have *already* done by making *little* changes," Paula advised. Then she showed Susan how to add a line to the leaves here, a dab of shadow to the petals there, a few dots of intense color to the centers. They were small changes, but they had a significant effect.

A few years later, Susan was marketing a successful line of hand-painted hardware. She saw the value of Paula's little-by-little revisions and suggestions and began applying this approach to her home, to her relationships, to nearly everything she does.

*Small changes are more consistent with human nature and evolution.* Assuming Darwin was correct, evolution demonstrates that small changes over a long period of time have made us vastly different from our prehistoric ancestors. While we do not suggest that anyone wait eons for improvement, we will show how cultivating a small change in a daily habit can build to a significant change over time. Consider the example of Trudy.

Trudy was single and lived with her mother. After her mother died, grief-stricken Trudy went for a short walk. While the walk left her somewhat out of breath, it cleared her head and lifted her spirits. The next day Trudy took another short walk around her neighborhood. Again, she found herself feeling better afterward.

In time Trudy no longer had to say "I think I'll take a walk to feel better." She had acquired the habit of walking before or after dinner each day. This new habit brought Trudy greater clarity, less tension, and a broader perspective. By the way, two years later Trudy was fifty-five pounds lighter, and much happier with her body and her life.

*Small change is a better way to a better you.* Our method of self-improvement advocates a soft touch. It doesn't require tremendous self-discipline or radical changes and thus offers you a more *pleasant* journey of self-improvement. Its perspective offers greater self-acceptance, the promise of sustained success, and the motivation to be both realistic and optimistic about change. The slow but steady tortoise enjoyed the journey, along with the satisfaction of winning the race.

*Small changes provide multiple benefits.* Making small changes can be fun. Small changes can provide a sense of accomplishment for people who think they lack willpower. Small changes foster self-acceptance for people who criticize themselves for failing to make big changes. Small changes make it possible to modify a pleasurable habit rather than give it up altogether. And for those who see life as a series of lessons and opportunities—not a series of mistakes and inadequacies—small changes are a great way to put this philosophy into practice.

Aiming for big changes that are difficult to accomplish often results in no change at all. Worse, you may be left with a sense of failure and inadequacy that can be painful and unwarranted. A small change is *always* better than no change at all. Modest success is *always* better than failure and pain. By acquiring the habit of making small changes, you can build those moderate successes into dramatic results—because small changes *will* add up.

With an emphasis on the importance of daily habits, and some simple recipes for improving them, we offer you a fresh perspective on the timeless quest for sustainable self-improvement—a simple, powerful, better way to a better you.

# I. How to Apply Small Change to Your Life

## RULE 1: Look Closely at What You Do Every Day.

Put your change in a piggy bank every single day and watch it steadily accumulate. Put your change in only occasionally, and it still adds up, just not as fast. The same holds true for the changes we make in our lives. Change something in your daily life, and you will see the benefits steadily accumulate. Change something you do occasionally, and it too will bring benefits, just not as fast.

That is why our daily habits have such significant effects. It is also why daily habits can work in reverse. For example, occasional hot fudge sundaes will not add up (you know where) as fast as daily hot fudge sundaes.

Don't take just our advice on this. Listen to Aristotle, who wisely observed that our daily habits and behaviors are the building blocks of our lives: "We are what we repeatedly do," he advised. "Excellence, then, is not an act, but a habit."

**IT IS EASIEST** to remember to make a change when it is something you do every day. And of course, when you can remember the change you want to make, you are more likely to sustain the change until it becomes a habit. And once a change becomes a habit, it is behavior you are likely to keep doing for a long time. If you are always misplacing your house key and focus on remembering to put it in the same place every time you use it, in time where you put it will become habit, one you are unlikely to break.

Chapters 2 through 6 of this book look at some of the most common areas of everyday life. In each chapter we offer numerous suggestions for changes. Our advice is to look first at daily habits, at least as you embark on this journey of self-improvement. And by all means, don't limit your change to our suggestions.

Occasionally, we suggest a change that occurs less frequently in your life, because small change isn't a rigid system. We offer them because certain changes, while small, can still make a big difference in your life over time.

When Larry officiates at weddings, he likes to remind couples that "life unfolds one moment at a time; the path is traveled one step at a time." What you do every day carries you along that road that is your life. Making a small change does not simply change one step; it changes the entire journey.

Break a bad habit, and with one small step you begin to put your life back on course. Develop new habits, and take your life in a fresh direction. Aiming at small changes, you are less likely to fail. And when you focus your change on a daily habit, the opportunity, when you do forget, presents itself again the very next day.

Small change is a gentle system of self-improvement. We are not selling you a new you or a new journey. We are helping you tweak the one you already have. (Secretly, we think it is the way you were meant to be anyway.) People with big "issues" may need new vehicles, new maps, and new destinations, but our experience shows us that all that most people need is to refine who they already are and think about how they are getting where they are already going. Focus on what you are doing every day, and your life will stay in much sharper focus.

## RULE 2: Make Only One Change at a Time.

Imagine putting *one* New Year's resolution on your list—only *one.* Consider how much easier it is to concentrate on only one, to remember only one, to work on only one small change. Consider, too, that if you fail to make that one small change, you face just a minor setback—not the pain of failing to achieve the big personal transformation that you may have already announced to the world!

Remembering to make only one small change requires a small effort—perhaps a few "triggers" for your memory, such as a note next to your bed or on the bathroom mirror, maybe another in your daily calendar, on your computer, or on the refrigerator door. Another trigger might be to link the change to a regular part of your daily routine, such as driving your car, going to the bathroom, or eating a meal. Easy enough.

It may also seem easy enough to feel you can handle more than one change at a time, especially when you think you are "on a roll" in self-improvement. However, the system works best when you focus on only one small change at a time. Consider Aesop's fable about the race between the tortoise and the hare. Slow and steady won the race for Tortoise; fast and distracted lost it for Hare.

And hey—remember the KISS formula? (Keep It Simple, Stupid.) One small change at a time is a KISS formula. We live in busy times, with busy careers, busy family lives, busy, busy, busy. Why add more busy-ness to an already busy life? Why not keep self-improvement simple?

We are not saying that you can't make a lot of changes—in fact, we hope that you will make many throughout your life. We simply believe that your best chance for succeeding is to focus on *one small change* at a time.

Need more convincing? Consider this metaphor. It is difficult to push a rock uphill but much easier to carry a small stone up a mountain. Big makeovers, involving many changes in deep-seated habits, are like heavy rocks. When you keep your change small, like the stone, you have a better chance for long-term success.

On the other hand, don't think because it is *only* one small change, it isn't a Big Deal. Look at the larger picture, the timeline of your life. Although you make only one change at a time, you will do this many, many times, hopefully, over the course of your life. Each change adds up, and all the changes together add up. Our son and daughter-in-law live atop a steep hill in San Francisco. The easiest way to walk up the hill is to take the avenue with the built-in stairs. Similarly, self-improvement is easiest when taken one step at a time.

**WHEN ARE YOU READY** to move on to your next change? We offer no hard-and-fast rule for this, since some changes are easier to make than others. Naturally, the more motivation, self-discipline, mindfulness, and ability to remember a change you have, the less time it will take you. In general, our advice is to be flexible, but think in terms of weeks. Every few weeks, or at least every month or so, start a new change.

Susan finds it easiest to start a new change at the start of each month. Larry makes a new change whenever he feels ready. You may find a different, perhaps more creative method for moving on. This is not a rigid system, after all, but a gentle method of self-improvement.

Some people will make a dozen or more changes in a year while others will make just six or eight. Doesn't matter. Each change is a small step in self-improvement. Each change is good. Each change will add up.

**CHANGING A HABIT** is like a classic drama with its standard three acts. Sustainable change has a clear beginning, middle, and end.

**ACT 1.** Look closely at your life to identify a habit or pattern that you know you want to change.

**ACT 2.** Make the change.

**ACT 3.** Sustain the change and reap the benefits.

By the time the curtain falls, your change should be a habit—and no longer in need of all your attention. Sustaining a change can be difficult, as anyone who has lost weight, stopped smoking, or started a new exercise program can attest. By giving yourself at least several weeks before starting the next change, you give the first change a chance to become a habit—hopefully, a lifelong habit.

**YOU MAY BELIEVE** that many of the changes we propose seem so easy you could handle more than one at a time. We suggest patience. Keep a list, perhaps. Move on when you are ready. If you follow Susan's program of one change per month, you can schedule them on your calendar (or not). By following her model, in five years you can make sixty *sustainable* changes. If you try to do too much too quickly, you may lose steam and fail to make any.

**BE REALISTIC** about change. No matter how small the change, bad habits die hard. New habits can take time and perseverance. Accept that some changes may not stick on your first (or third) effort. It is okay. It takes the average smoker five to six attempts before successfully quitting. Surely you can cut yourself some slack and allow more than one attempt to break an ingrained habit like mindless munching or a heavy foot on the gas pedal.

Sometimes, too, you will make a small change, only to discover weeks, months, or even years later that you have forgotten the change and reverted back to your old ways. Again, be kind to yourself and just try again. And again, if need be. (Clearly, it helps to be an optimist.)

**IT WOULD BE EASY** to feel overexcited by the scores of suggestions in this book and get zealous about making as many changes as you want as fast as you can. This kind of enthusiasm, while admirable, misses an important point: you are not as far off course as you think.

Small change requires awareness of how you are living your life. It keeps you from remaining on "automatic pilot," mindlessly following the same routine, day after day, year after year. But it does not encourage you to completely dismantle your routine. Rather, the small change approach to self-improvement should inspire you to seek balance in your life—balance between the journey and the destination, between improving yourself and accepting the person you already are. *One change at a time.* What could be easier than that?

## RULE 3: Make Small Change a Constant in Your Life.

Does a cellist ever stop practicing her cello? An artist stop exploring her art? An athlete stop working at his game? A couple stop developing their relationship? A home or garden stop needing improvements? We rest our case. Make small change a constant in your life, and you will continue to make your life better . . . and better . . . and better.

Instruments tuned on a regular basis are easier to tune. Exercise is easier when you are in the habit of doing it. If you are in the habit of change, changing is easier. Being in the habit of constant change keeps you flexible and open-minded, mindful and diligent—all building blocks of self-improvement. Again, make small change a constant in your life, and your life will always be improving.

. . .

**OUR IDEA** of using small changes for self-improvement grew out of Larry's teachings. Since 1978 we have owned an old church building on the village green of a bucolic little midwestern town. In this charming (and *very* conservative) setting, Larry runs a holistic center, teaches yoga, and performs weddings and other ceremonies. In the building we also have a nursery school, a synagogue, and a space where we host art shows, poetry readings, concerts, vegetarian potlucks . . . and it's really too complicated to explain in one paragraph, let alone one very long sentence.

Larry likes change. He acquires new habits the way other people acquire new possessions, and over the years has used his method of small change to improve his diet, health, relationships, golf game, and yadda yadda yadda.

Susan never liked much change in her life. She has lived in the same house (with Larry and children) and intends to stay there—forever (she even entertains the possibility of being a ghost there someday). Still, Susan understands that change is unavoidable and that self-improvement yields numerous rewards. She became hooked on small change the year she trimmed her New Year's list to just one resolution—and discovered how easy it was to keep that one. (That year it was getting in the habit of using her rearview mirror when driving.)

Soon, though, Susan saw that she could handle change on a regular basis—and that doing so was even fun (and a relief for all the other drivers on the road).

Making small changes works for anyone—for those like Larry, who relish change, and for those like Susan, who see its value, even if they haven't always loved doing it.

Here's our point. One small change at a time may not seem like much. Nor is it a quick fix for a major problem in your life. But constant change—continually adding one small change to another small change to another and another—puts you in the "habit" of breaking habits and acquiring new ones by strengthening your willpower, resolve, and awareness. In this way, too, success in your practice of making small changes will give you the confidence and strength you need when life does demand big changes.

Small change is not going to transform you into a new person overnight, because with small change, we aren't redefining ourselves but rather are *refining* ourselves. Make one small change a month, though, and watch yourself dramatically improve who you already are—over time.

Making small change a constant helps you become aware of what you are doing and develop a perspective on the long-term effects. You will be better able to "see" the larger picture and the cumulative consequences of your choices.

The very practice of looking at your habits, remembering your current small change, and gaining a broad perspective on your behavior brings control to your thoughts and actions—in the gentlest of ways. Indeed, this awareness may end up being the most important benefit of all. And the mindfulness and self-control you develop over time may prevent bad habits from creeping into your life in the first place.

What happens if you forget or fail to make the small change you committed to making? Well, now, do you stop flossing altogether because you miss a few weeks? Do you end the quest for a healthier lifestyle because you mess up on a few meals? Do you go home because you made a wrong turn in the road? Do you give up because you fail a few times? No! You can begin anew for as many times as you need. Make the trying constant. Make small change constant. Keep the process going as long as you live.

**BEFORE WE FINISH** this section, it is time to make an important point. *Small change is about constantly improving* your *life, not forcing change onto someone else for your benefit.* No doubt many of the changes you will make have a positive effect on others, especially on people close to you. In addition, changes such as staying in touch may require cooperation from another person. Other changes, such as improving your vocabulary or manners, can benefit from another person's involvement.

If you choose to embrace this system of self-improvement in tandem with another person, you can give each other encouragement and help, regardless of whether you both work on the same change or on different changes. Together you can even brainstorm new changes for each other. The caveat here is obvious, though. Be careful not to use small change as an excuse to manipulate or coerce someone else into changing. Nor should small change be used as a license to criticize or nag.

**IN SHORT,** making small changes, one at a time, makes change a constant. And constantly improving your life is, in itself, a habit. Remember the poem by William Makepeace Thackeray?

> Sow a thought and reap an act;
> Sow an act and reap a habit;
> Sow a habit and reap a character;
> Sow a character and reap a destiny.

Keep sowing small changes to reap the destiny you want.

## RULE 4: Trust the Power of Small Change, and Remember, It Will Add Up.

Small change adds up—over time, not overnight! You may get immediate satisfaction out of certain changes. But with many changes, the effects accumulate slowly, and the bigger payoffs occur in the future, maybe even far in the future. Our advice is to be realistic about change and maintain a healthy perspective toward it. Small change is a method of self-improvement that requires trust in its power to incrementally improve your life.

Some changes may also require the ability to delay gratification, to keep your eye on the prize while you make small changes in the present.

Here is a story to ponder. In a well-known study of four-year-olds, a teacher presented each child with a choice: get a treat (one marshmallow) right away or wait until the teacher returned from an errand and get an extra marshmallow for being patient. Two-thirds of the children postponed the pleasure of eating one marshmallow for the chance to double that pleasure. The results of a follow-up study when the children reached adolescence were even more interesting. The children who could delay gratification at age four showed the greatest academic success later. The four-year-olds' ability to delay gratification was a better indicator of future school success than were standardized tests.

Small change has a reward—but, as in the previous study, you have to trust that it will be there for you in the future. And to get the reward, you have to exercise some willpower and resist the temptation to fall into a familiar behavior pattern.

To see the larger picture, especially the distant future, it helps to understand how a change is going to add up. Sometimes you can actually do mathematical calculations, as we have done for a number of small changes throughout these chapters. For other changes, the effects are less calculable but nevertheless imaginable. At age twenty, your skin probably looks like that of every other twenty-year-old. Protect your skin from too much sun, though, and at age sixty-five, your face will have fewer wrinkles and discolored areas and you will be less likely to get skin cancer than your perpetually tanned friends.

Read a few pages of a book each day, and in a year you may complete two or three books. This may not sound like much, but it only takes one great book to have a lasting impression on your life. Read those few pages every night for the rest of your life, however, and you can gain immeasurable knowledge, wisdom, and entertainment.

Start substituting an apple (80 calories) for a small muffin (140 calories) as a morning snack a few days a week at age forty. By age seventy-five you will have consumed nearly five hundred thousand (a half million!) fewer calories and have fewer pounds around your hips or midriff. And if you were substituting the apple for a glazed donut (250 calories), you would save 2 million calories. Now there's a small change that adds up!

Plant a sapling and wait a few years. You will have a tree ready for a bird feeder. Wait a decade, and your tree will give you ample shade. In a generation your tree will be sturdy enough to support a swing, a tree house, or the end of a hammock. When you trust in the power of small change, you plant seeds of change, one at a time, and allow them to grow into better health, better relationships, better minds, better spirits, better lives. We cannot promise that small change will give you a good life—no one can. But we can promise that you will live a better life, a more satisfying life, a happier life, as a result.

Small change to self-improvement is slow and steady, gentle and easy. Very slow and steady. Very gentle and easy.

Big problems are no excuse to avoid small change. In fact, many big problems can benefit by finding small changes that can improve them, one small step at a time. At the very least, by improving other areas of your life, a big problem may loosen its grip on you. So, regardless of whether you have a troubled past, a difficult family relationship, or a chronic condition, small change has the power to improve your life—especially when you see how easy it is to make small changes, one at a time.

The secret to staying on course is being able to visualize your destination. So, again, no excuses. If you want small change to work, you need to muster up a small amount (small, we repeat) of self-control, self-discipline, resolve, and confidence, a small amount of patience and optimism, and a great big dose of trust in the power of small change to make a big difference in your life.

## RULE 5: Enjoy Making Small Changes.

If you can make small change fun, keeping a lighthearted perspective and a sense of humor about it, you will have the best chance of succeeding at making small changes and of making small changing a permanent part of your life. Small change is easy, except for one little requirement—actually *remembering* the change you decided to make. (Isn't that always the hardest part of New Year's resolutions?) We can assure you, however, that the easiest rule is this: enjoy making your small changes.

The small changes we recommend throughout the book are always little tuneups, never major overhauls. The joy and success you experience will come most easily if you keep a lighthearted outlook and a sense of humor on the quest for self-improvement.

Remember: small change works best when you make it fun, keep it lighthearted, and enjoy the process. And now that you understand all the rules, good luck—and get going!

# 2. Small Changes for Better Health

Nowhere is the prospect for self-improvement through small change more certain than in the daily habits that relate to your physical health. In this chapter you will find suggestions for improving everything from your breathing and posture to your eating and hygiene habits.

It is easy to read these suggestions, though, and be overwhelmed—by all the bad habits you have and the good ones you don't have! Susan had one of these existential moments one day while she was working on the section about exercise, which she had neglected to do—at all—during our long winter.

By the time the book was complete, she had acquired several new health habits, including giving up on chewing ice (bad, can crack your teeth) and vowing to floss regularly (good). Larry, who is quite a health and fitness buff, didn't find as many small changes to make in this area. Still, he was inspired to replace soda with water at dinnertime (nice). Max, a young friend who read the section on smoking, quit (excellent).

We are confident that you will find at least a few small changes you can make over time. And confident, too, that you will make them *one at a time.* Because that is one of the secrets to making small change work for you.

## Catch Your Breath

Make a small change in the way you breathe? Isn't breathing the most natural thing we can do? The reason for starting here is because breathing is *the most important activity* in your life. The most important.

Let's get this straight. The average person can survive without food for many weeks. You can do without water for many days. But you can do without oxygen for only a few minutes.

Here is how it works. Every cell in our body is a tiny engine. As in a car or furnace, within each cell oxygen mixes with fuel, and its combustion produces energy.

In your body the rate at which that combustion occurs is known as your metabolism.

The fuel for your car may be gasoline, and for your furnace it is probably natural gas or oil. For your cells, the fuel is fat and carbohydrates. But as with furnaces and combustion engines, it is oxygen that drives the process. (Remember, oxygen plus fuel combusts to give you energy.) Oxygen is required to extract the energy from any fuel. Cut off the supply of air, and a car screeches to a halt, a furnace goes cold, a cell dies. Cut off air for only a few minutes, and a person dies.

Athletes know that refining their breathing techniques can enhance performance significantly. For centuries, yogis have taught that the breath is the key to unlocking powers in the body and mind. In their quest to find the perfect fuel/oxygen ratio for optimal performance, race car drivers experiment with their carburetors. Is there a message here for us, too?

Breath is a critical component of energy, and also participates in two other essential aspects of our lives—our emotional state and our consciousness. Emotions—such as anger, sadness, laughter, fear, and relaxation—are associated with specific breathing patterns. In a state of anger, for example, the body produces more adrenaline, a hormone that speeds up breathing. By consciously changing the way you are breathing (such as slowing it down by counting the breaths), you can affect your emotional state and become less angry.

Breathing also affects our awareness. When we are asleep, our breathing is automatic; we do not notice it. When, however, we are totally alert, as when we are getting ready to dive off a high board into a pool, receive an award, or prepare to meditate, we are conscious of our breathing and inclined to control it, either by deepening our inhales, holding our breath, slowing down our exhales, or, as in meditation, taking control of the whole process.

Another way breathing puts us in the present, so to speak, is by its connection to the sense of smell, which helps us to savor our food, appreciate fresh air on a clear day, or get motivated to change a baby's diaper!

**WANT TO ADD** something to your daily routine that can help you release stress, produce more energy, help you be more creative, and expand your consciousness? Try a dose of LSD (low, slow, deep) breathing—the body's natural high.

**BREATHE LOW.** Most of us breathe too high in the chest, sometimes in an effort to hold in the stomach for cosmetic reasons. To breathe deeply, though, we need to make better use of all of the muscles involved, in order to utilize the full capacity of our lungs. This means letting our bellies expand when we inhale to allow the lower lungs to get into the act.

**BREATHE SLOW.** Most of us breathe too quickly, as if our fast-paced lives demand fast-paced breathing.

**BREATH DEEP.** Most of us are taking breaths that are too shallow, often because of the stress in our lives.

**REMEMBER:** Breathe low. Breathe slow. Breathe deep.

Entire books have been written about how to breathe. To keep this simple, however, just imagine filling a pitcher with water.

**INHALE:**

Breathe low, filling your lungs from the bottom up (as water fills a pitcher).

Breathe slow, filling your lungs slowly, carefully, mindfully.

Breathe deep, filling your lungs as completely as possible.

**EXHALE:** Slowly exhale, from the top of the lungs down to the bottom (a pitcher is emptied from the top down), using your abdomen to squeeze out as much air as possible, in preparation for the next LSD inhale.

Breathing practice can be done anywhere, any time.

Find something, a "trigger," to remind you to practice your LSD breathing, perhaps:

When you first wake up
Before you fall asleep (unless this gives you too much energy)
Before eating
Every time you yawn (the body's not-so-subtle hint it needs a deep breath)
Waiting for a traffic light to turn green (this is Larry's advice for reducing road rage)
When sitting on the john
*Any* time you remember

If you want to slow down the pace of your life, reduce the stress in it, gain more energy, be more creative, concentrate better, and be more "present," do LSD breathing for at least one or two minutes twice a day. In a year, this adds up to twenty-four hours of conscious breathing. Improve your breathing, and you will find yourself improving your life at the same time.

## Change One Meal

It's time to talk about something we do every day—eat. What we eat, when we eat, why we eat, and how much we eat all affect our well-being. Poor eating habits lead to added weight, low energy, disease, guilt, and low self-esteem. Good eating habits are, well, good. Clearly, small changes at mealtime can pay big dividends over time.

Let's do some math. The average person eats two to three meals a day, or fourteen to twenty-one meals a week, or about one thousand meals a year, or ten thousand meals per decade—seventy-five thousand to one hundred thousand meals if you live to a ripe old age.

We say: don't change all those meals at once (what an overwhelming task!). Most diets require numerous (and often big) changes. Is it any wonder, with so many changes, why people have so much difficulty sustaining a diet? Or why a small slip can sabotage the whole program?

Our approach is to divide and conquer. Pick one meal: breakfast, lunch, or dinner. Take one month to focus on making one healthful change in that one meal. (*One* sustainable change in *only one* meal changes one-third of all the meals you eat and many thousands of meals over the rest of your life.)

If you start with breakfast, consider this story. Our friend Annie Mae worked as a housekeeper at a busy college sorority house. She never ate breakfast because, like many people, she did not experience morning hunger, even after eight to twelve hours of fasting (basically what our bodies do overnight). By midmorning, however, Annie Mae always had a headache, and by midafternoon she was exhausted. Susan suggested that she try eating some cheese on crackers or toast with her morning coffee.

Right away Annie Mae's headaches disappeared, her fatigue disappeared, and for the next forty years she continued the habit of eating a small portion of protein every morning and enjoying the benefits. As we write this book she is eighty-six, fit as a fiddle, and still pontificating on the value of bending over to work in the garden. She does not believe in getting down on her hands and knees. Says that is too easy and she'd miss the stretch.

Like Annie Mae, if you don't eat an early breakfast, consider eating a small midmorning meal—a protein snack of a handful of nuts or seeds, a glass of milk or container of yogurt, a tablespoon or two of peanut butter, a slice of turkey or wedge of cheese. Better yet, though, get in the habit of eating a wholesome breakfast. One study showed that a lifetime of eating a healthy daily breakfast cut the risk of both obesity and diabetes in half. Your body needs fuel, especially after sleeping all night. A healthy breakfast does not add excess weight. Dinner and snacks take care of that.

Then there's lunch. Much of the world makes this the big meal. The wisdom here is that a good chunk of time is left in the day to burn this fuel. A good balanced meal at the middle of the day energizes your afternoon. Lunch needs protein and complex carbohydrates, not excess sugar, fat, grease, or super-sized portions. A healthy sandwich, perhaps with a cup of soup, a vegetable, or a salad can take you a long way here. If you look at your lunch habits, you will know what changes can be made.

Finally, there's dinner—your best opportunity to lighten up your eating. Unless you are a night owl (and this is actually lunch for you), dinnertime leaves insufficient time in the day to burn off much fuel. Eat too much at dinner, therefore, and you store the unused energy for future use—a gentle euphemism for excess fat tucked away in thighs, hips, waists, arms, and buttocks.

Dinner is an excellent place to consider cutting your portions to, say, fist size. When you eat out, get in the habit of eating only half the main course and taking the rest home. Or split the main course with someone else. One of our habits is to order an appetizer as our main course. You may save money as well. Last, when your dinner is take-out, get in the habit of putting half the food in the refrigerator—*before* you take the first bite.

Now, we are betting that we do not have to tell you all the flaws of your current diet. By asking you to look at only one of your meals, we are confident that you can find something to change. In case you can't, here are some more suggestions.

*Make substitutions.* Switch from butter to flax seed oil, from blue cheese or ranch dressing to olive oil and vinegar. On your bagel substitute brie, which contains more protein than cream cheese or butter. Substitute whole grains for refined, poultry or fish for meat, roasted for fried, a two-egg for a three-egg omelet.

Switch from croutons to sunflower seeds on your salad, from candy to granola bars or fruit, from chips to air-popped popcorn, from soda to sparkling water, from sour cream to yogurt, from french fries to baked potatoes, from eating late dinners to eating early suppers.

Take a daily vitamin while reading the daily news; add brewer's yeast or protein powder to your morning juice; add more vegetables to your lunch or dinner.

*Get artistic about one meal.* We don't mean presentation here (although switching to nice china or arranging your food artfully for one meal is a great idea). We mean, make sure that one meal of the day is as colorful as you can get. Give up white—white sugar, white bread, white pasta, white butter, and white starchy anything—and add as much color as possible with vegetables or fruits.

*Eat fish on Fridays,* even if you're Muslim, Jewish, Buddhist, or a Jewish Buddhist. Several recent studies have demonstrated that eating fish once a week or more yields a host of benefits: healthier arteries, reduced risk of heart attack and stroke, and perhaps lower risk of dementia.

The main point here is to make only one change in one meal at a time. You pick the meal. Or, as in the case of breakfast, start eating the meal. In short, learn to make healthier substitutes, learn to eat healthier portions, learn to like fish, and learn to eat a more *naturally* colorful diet (iced cakes, while gorgeous, don't count). Sustain one small change every now and then in just one meal, and over your lifetime you will have changed thousands of meals.

## Slow Down and Enjoy Your Food

Want to make a small change that will yield *huge* results? *Slow down and enjoy your food.* Trust us, though, this is one of those small changes that is difficult to remember, and takes a lot of practice, especially if you are accustomed to eating on the run, eating while standing up, or talking fast. (For some reason, fast talkers seem to be fast eaters, too.)

Eating more slowly yields great benefits for the effort. First, eating slowly gives your brain sufficient time to know that you have eaten enough, which helps keep you from overeating. When Larry's brother was an adolescent, he actually lost thirty-five pounds *just by chewing more thoroughly and eating more slowly.* And thirty-five years later, although Marc has to work at maintaining his weight, he has never since been seriously overweight.

Second, eating more slowly helps you get more pleasure from your food. It helps you savor the flavor and perhaps, the presentation; it allows you to appreciate the texture, aroma, and joy of the food.

Remember what we said about deep breathing earlier? Breathing deeply not only slows you down but allows you to savor your food more, since the enjoyment of food has much to do with how it smells and tastes, which is closely connected to breathing.

**AT FIRST,** eating more slowly may take concentration, self-control, and awareness until it becomes a new habit. Here are some helpful hints.

One idea is to time your meals to see whether you need to slow down or not. Put the timer on fifteen to twenty minutes for breakfast or lunch; twenty-five minutes for dinner. Now eat. If the timer goes off before you are finished, you pass the test. If, however, you always finish before the timer sounds, especially for a three-course dinner, you might want to consider slowing down.

Of course, the most common advice for slowing down is to chew more slowly. Another way to eat more slowly is to get in the habit of periodically putting down your fork. Or put less food on your fork or spoon. In addition, whenever you can, eat with a fork and knife—even sandwiches or pizza—instead of your fingers. Naturally, it takes longer, but that is the whole point here.

If you regard eating as dining and not just fueling up that body of yours, you will find it easier to justify more time eating. Dining alone? Put on soft music. Or read. Use your good china. Anything that makes you feel you are elevating eating to dining will probably slow you down.

One way to slow down when eating with others is to get in the habit of pacing yourself to the slowest person at the table. If you are eating with someone else, talk more. Back-and-forth conversation is a great way to slow down. In our house, by the way, we never use eating time for working out relationship problems, disciplining our children, or anything else unpleasant. Doing so risks giving those present a lifetime of indigestion. It also teaches them to eat quickly in order to get away from the table sooner.

**TO BECOME MORE** mindful about dining and more grateful about the food you eat, try this small but powerful change. *Contemplate your food before eating it,* either before the entire meal or as you pick up each bite.

We know that you know that people are starving everywhere in the world, or at least going to sleep hungry. If you don't feel fortunate to be eating when thirty million children die of starvation every single year, and millions more go to sleep hungry, then get a life. Seriously, before sitting down to any meal, including a snack, first remind yourself how lucky you are to be eating anything at all, let alone eating food you like. Simple enough.

Here are some other mealtime small changes you can choose to make into habits.

Say a prayer, either a ritual prayer from an organized religion or one you write yourself.
Be silent for a minute or so.
Take a few deep breaths before eating.
Hold hands with others at the table.
Sing a song or recite a verse.
In the evening, get in the habit of eating with the lights dimmed, by candlelight, or with soft music.

While we are on the subject of eating, we (okay, Susan) can't help but suggest a few changes in the *way* you may be eating. Have you gotten into the habit of talking while chewing? Not good. Truthfully, it is as bad as chewing with your mouth open, and maybe worse, because in addition to aesthetic considerations, talking while chewing increases the chance that you may swallow your food down the wrong pipe and choke. (So what if the chances of choking are slim—Larry once rescued a woman who had nearly choked to death on a large piece of meat she swallowed while talking.)

Here are four easy habits to clean up your manners.

Chew with your mouth closed.
Use your napkin (but not for blowing your nose).

Keep your elbows off the table.

Use your fingers sparingly (to pick *up* the sandwich, not to *pick apart* the sandwich; to take the roll out of the bread basket, not to pass the roll to someone else).

If this talk about manners seems pretentious, then consider this: like thank-you notes, good manners won't win you friends, jobs, or much else, but bad manners can lose them for you. Sorry, that's life. You may be in good company if you have family or friends with less than perfect manners. But you can *become* better company when you make a small change in the way you eat—even when dining alone.

## Scrutinize Your Snacks

Mindless munching—that's what a lot of us are in the habit of doing. Snacking has probably reached an all-time high in popularity. We eat on the run, and we eat when we are bored. We eat while we watch TV, drive, attend sporting events, and go to the movies.

Now Larry has a theory. (Mind you, it is untested—

and only a theory.) Larry's Three-Day Donut Theory is this: *physiological addictions are formed in three days.* Here is his corollary: those same addictions can be overcome, at least physiologically, in (as little as) three days.

Consider the following scenario.

**DAY 1: THE BEGINNING.** Eat a donut at 10 a.m. Your body marshals its resources and metabolizes the donut. You enjoy a burst of energy as the sugar, converted to glucose, enters the bloodstream.

**DAY 2: THE DEFINING MOMENT.** It is 10 a.m. Your body is on guard, wondering whether it will get the same sugar rush. You eat a donut. The body responds to the burst of energy.

**DAY 3: THE HABIT.** Your body has now learned what to expect and is *eagerly* awaiting its 10 a.m. sugary snack. Not to be caught off guard, it begins getting ready around 9:30 by preparing the gastric juices and other chemicals required to metabolize the anticipated donut. This preparation, in fact, is what causes your feeling of hunger (the body's not-so-subtle demand for its anticipated donut fix). Don't eat the donut, and the body will have to reabsorb the chemicals it has produced and will dispute your decision through headaches, irritability, or fatigue. Or eat the donut, and congratulate yourself—for giving your body a sugar addiction—in just three days. Why not add a cup of coffee and create a caffeine addiction as well?

To break your physical addiction, you must reverse the process.

**DAY 1: THE CRAVING.** It is 10:00 a.m. The body is irritable, maybe suffering from a headache, hunger pain, or fatigue. It craves that sugar or caffeine. Don't give in! Don't eat the donut! Don't drink the coffee! Suffer! (Try taking an aspirin or a brisk walk.) Bear in mind: *This too shall pass.*

**DAY 2: BETTER BUT NOT GOOD.** No donut, no coffee. The body will still send you its message that it is time for some sugar or caffeine, but at least it is not sure they will be coming. Relax, the worst is now over.

**DAY 3: GOING, GOING, GONE.** Gone is the physical addiction. The body no longer gets ready in advance and then demands its fix. At least physiologically, your addiction has been brought under control. (Overcoming the psychological addiction can take much longer.)

If you subscribe to Larry's theory, here is the good news on snacks. You *can* have them, but not two or three days in a row at the same time of day. As the previous scenario shows, day 1 isn't the problem—day 2 is.

Want to make a change that will really add up over time? Switch soda and sweets from a daily habit to a sometime treat. There's even a secondary reward for such self-control: consuming them only occasionally takes the "mindless" out of mindless munching, which allows you to savor and enjoy treats more when you do have them. This restores them to a "treat" status. Achieving this self-control adds still another level of satisfaction and accomplishment.

**FOR SOME PEOPLE,** snacking is essential. For anyone, adding healthier snacks to their diet is an improvement. For example, consider substituting:

Nuts and seeds for cookies and cake
Popcorn for chips
Yogurt or a chunk of cheese for ice cream
Smaller bags of food for larger bags of food
Herbal tea for caffeine drinks
Berries for candy
Water for soda

To refine these choices even more, get in the habit of asking yourself why you crave the snack. Are you hungry? Tired? Thirsty? Bored? Nervous? Addicted? Food gives us energy, but if you are tired, you may want to consider resting instead. In addition, increasing the protein in your snack and decreasing the sugar will provide a longer term energy boost.

Many of us have acquired the habit of snacking when we are just thirsty. Of course, the best thirst quencher is water. You could also get in the habit of a "wet" snack, such as cucumbers, apples, or pears or a natural fruit juice popsicle.

**A SMALL** but important change to consider is the nighttime snack. It is best to avoid eating solid foods after dinner, or at least to remain snack free for the three hours before bedtime. At night, especially after a late dinner, the body lacks the time it needs to work off the energy derived from a big meal. And eating solid food late at night puts a burden on the digestive system, which can disturb your sleep.

**REMEMBER,** you are going to make only one small change at a time. Don't choose to work on mindless munching expecting to shed a million zillion pounds (because that may take a big change). Choose it because you will lose some. Choose it because it will bring more awareness and self-control to your life. Choose it because it is healthier. The fruit that replaces donuts may actually get you one less clogged artery in life—and that's a pretty good return on your effort, isn't it?

## No Time to Exercise?

Many questions swirl around the issue of exercise. Take the amount of exercise you need. The most recent advice is to get an hour each day. Other common advice is to get in twenty to thirty minutes three times a week. Every fitness guru has a new system, a new book, a new infomercial. One new system promotes a small but extremely intense weight-lifting workout only eight to ten minutes long and only once a week. (Sounds good until you consider how sore your muscles are after this workout!)

Even advice about something as basic as walking is confusing. (And it sure got away from nature when we started walking on treadmills and in malls!) One popular approach is ten thousand steps a day. How far is that? With a small stride you will walk two to three miles, but if your stride is large you will walk up to five miles. Fast or slow? Arms swinging or not? Weights in your hands? How much? Oy vey!

Since we are *clearly* not exercise experts, we've decided to talk about dogs instead, hoping that you will see yourself in our presentation.

Dogs, like people, come in a variety of shapes and sizes, with differing life spans, energy levels, and needs for exercise. An Irish setter, for example, has a similar energy level to a Chihuahua, but the setter needs to be exercised vigorously. The Chihuahua requires only a little playtime.

So here is the basis of our exercise theory. First, *all* dogs require some exercise during the day. Second, some dogs, such as Border collies, require a great deal of exercise. Not just walk-around-the-block-on-a-leash exercise. We mean *running*—miles every day. Miles and miles. If a Border collie fails to get enough exercise, it may not become overweight, as perhaps a sluggish, overfed cocker spaniel will get. No, this high-energy (highly intelligent) Border collie is going to act quite dysfunctional—and tear apart your house!

Our *much* loved cockapoo, Skipper, in contrast, requires minimal exercise—running around the dining room table, bolting up and down the stairs, and a few short, very short, strolls until he does his business.

Now, here is the small change. Identify the dog-within-you; then eat and exercise accordingly. Most important, stop feeling guilty or bad about the dog you are not.

Remember, though, like *all* dogs, you need *some* exercise, probably every day. So why not do what most dogs do? Walk, play, and, *if it is in your nature,* swim or run.

**BECAUSE WALKING** uses a full fifty percent of 650 muscles, may we suggest walking as the easiest, most natural, most healthful exercise you can do? (If you cannot walk, swim. If you cannot swim, then walk in water.)

To make a big difference, carry weights while you walk. If you swing your arms to ear height, you increase the calories burned by as much as fifty percent. Swing them a few inches above your head and, baby, you will be cooking—and burning nearly *twice* as many calories.

**TO INCREASE** the exercise you get, here are some suggestions for small changes, many of which you may know but perhaps need to remind yourself to do.

**WALK WHILE YOU TALK.** Whenever possible, use a cordless phone or cell phone, or put a long cord on your phone; then walk or pace while you talk.

**TALK WHILE YOU WALK.** If you need to make a number of phone calls or one long call—for example, talking to your mother or best friend—plan to take a walk. To maximize your exercise, use earphones with your cell phone, which frees your arms so you can swing them—a small walking habit that adds up over time.

Get in the habit of parking as far away as you can, of taking stairs instead of escalators, walking instead of using the moving sidewalk, and getting off the bus stop one or two stops before or after your destination. (To be on the safe side, however, we do not suggest using isolated stairwells, except in an emergency.)

Like music and dancing? Then get in the habit of dancing to music on the radio, a CD, or a tape, or while you sing to yourself or just count out a beat. When alone, improvise a dance. With a partner, use the opportunity to have fun and improve your dancing. Our favorite work break is to put on some Latin or swing music and dance in our little foyer. We add some exercise to our day, and we also improve our dance skills. From these miniworkouts (they last just a song or two), we've added several new swing moves, the cha-cha, and the mambo. Give us another year or two, and we intend to know how to salsa. (Talk about small changes—it took us nearly fifteen years, but we can now do a pretty smooth jitterbug.)

Put more exercise into your cleaning routine by trying to do it more quickly or by running up and down the stairs or in and out of each room to retrieve your cleaning supplies. Most household mavens suggest that you carry supplies with you from room to room. Our system—while less efficient—results in more exercise, and that is what we are trying to accomplish here.

Want to stretch more? Start hanging your laundry outside to dry. Instead of storing essentials on the easiest-to-reach shelf, place them on the highest shelf so you have to stretch more often.

Finally, if you really want to ensure that you get enough exercise, get a dog. If that is not possible, offer to walk someone else's dog. (Walking puppies or unusual breeds are great ways to meet new people, while you also get exercise, and are compelled to go outdoors even in inclement weather.)

With the money you save by not hiring a personal trainer, you could probably buy any dog you want or pamper the free dog you get at the kennel. One helluva good deal—for you and the dog.

## Bathroom Yoga

We return to the theme of dogs. Instead of talking about exercise, though, we want to talk about its corollary—stretching. Ever watch a dog get up from a nap or deep sleep? Unless awakened suddenly, what a dog does first is *stretch.* There is great wisdom here, especially if you don't want to look like a stereotype of *old* age, hunched over, with one hand on your back, shuffling slowly and stiffly. The small change we are suggesting—stretching—will help you remain flexible.

Now one of the best ways to stretch your body, and experience a myriad of other benefits as well, is with yoga. We invite you to try a yoga class. Larry, who has been teaching yoga for over thirty years and likes all kinds of yoga (and he can get on swimmingly well with just about any dog), has developed a short but powerful yoga routine that can be done in the bathroom, at any countertop, with a doorknob, or at your desk. With his routine you don't need any yoga accouterments such as mats or special yoga clothing.

Stand about three feet away from the sink, or wherever you decide to do this routine. Place your feet hip distance apart and pointing forward (so you feel balanced and unlikely to slip). Bend forward from the waist, with your legs straight, and grab the sink. Now, draw your tailbone away from the sink and elongate your spine. Look up slightly at the faucet while trying to restore the natural curve in your lower spine, called the lumbar curve. Your heels should be six to eight inches closer to the sink than your tailbone, creating the angle shown in the illustration. This is a standing variation of a yoga pose called *Downward-Facing Dog.*

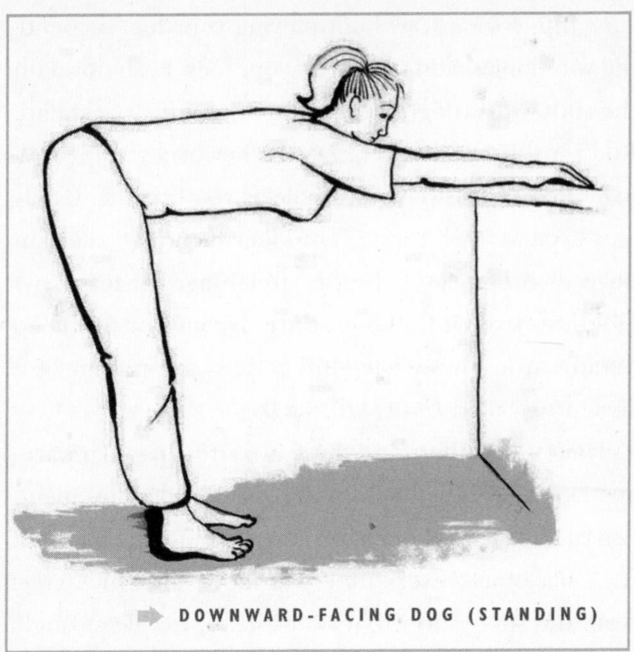

DOWNWARD-FACING DOG (STANDING)

(See, we mean it when we suggest you learn to stretch like a dog.)

Feel the spine opening and "releasing" (as they say in yoga). Feel the muscles stretching and "elongating" (as they also say in yoga). Breathe deeply, concentrating on the exhales. Hold this stretch for thirty to forty-five seconds, or through five deep breaths—and smile.

For the next stretch, stand up straight, then bring

your hips forward, without moving your feet or bending your knees, and rise up on your toes. Push down on the sink with straight arms, into a standing backbend. Roll your shoulders back, gaze at the corner of the ceiling, and emphasize your inhale as you breathe deeply and expand your chest. Try to feel as though the skin on your tummy and chest is stretching. (At least try.) Hold this stretch for about thirty seconds or five deep breaths. You guessed it—this pose is a variation of a yoga pose called *Upward-Facing Dog.*

Once you understand these two stretches—Upward- and Downward-Facing Dog—it is time to add movement. Alternate the two poses by moving your hips forward, then backward. Every time you move your hips away from the sink, into the forward bend, exhale strongly through your mouth. Every time you move your hips toward the sink, into the backbend, inhale strongly through your nose. Do this back and forth with strong exhales and strong inhales about ten times.

The final position in Bathroom Yoga is called *Mountain Pose.* (More detail on this pose is given in the next section, on posture.) Bring your feet together, toes and ankles touching, and stand as tall as possible. If you can, check your posture in the mirror. Your shoulders should line up over your hips, over your knees, over your ankles, and over the front of your heels. Take sev-

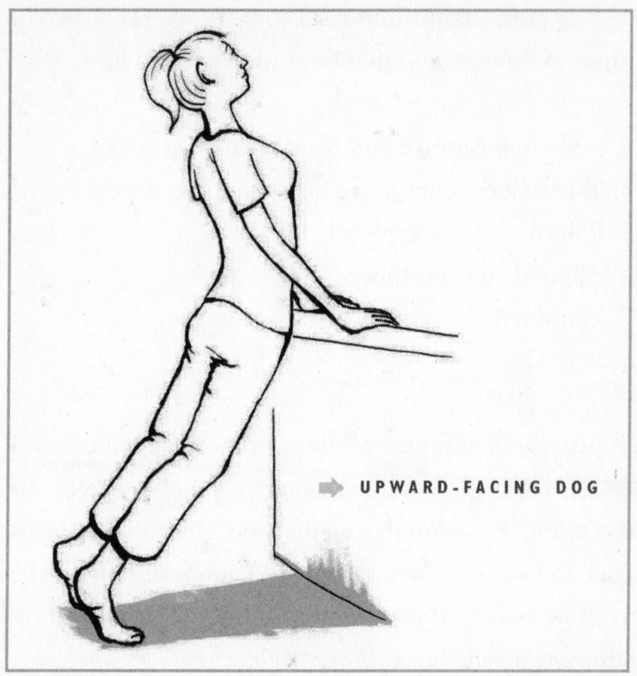

UPWARD-FACING DOG

eral deep breaths. Each inhale should feel as though you are lifting the top of your head away from the bottom of your heels—as if you are being stretched from both ends of your body. And, as in the other poses, don't forget to add the smile.

Standing tall in Mountain Pose will expand your chest, lift your spirits, add to your self-confidence, and give you a positive way to start your day.

This entire Bathroom Yoga routine takes only two to three minutes. Yet in that brief time you will have:

Stretched forward and backward
Taken deep, energizing breaths
Raised your energy level
Aligned your posture
Stood tall
Smiled

Just three minutes of Bathroom Yoga is powerful enough to give you all the energy you need to get your day going. Be assured, too, that you will *not* need to go back to bed! (You may *want* to but you won't *need* to.)

*Three minutes of yoga per day adds up to eighteen hours of stretching a year—as much yoga as you would get from six to ten days at a spa.*

You can use this yoga routine as a break at work or during a highway pit stop. You can use it when you return from work or shopping or anytime you feel as though you need a second wind to enjoy the rest of your day or evening. Every dog instinctively knows to stretch. Every athlete knows the value of stretching for peak performance. Our conclusion here is not that people are like dogs. No, it is that you, too, can make stretching as natural and as easy and as much a habit. And reap the same benefits.

## Improve Your Posture

One of Larry's favorite bumper stickers is "Gravity is not just a good idea, it's the law." Structures are strongest when everything is properly aligned. This goes for building blocks, towers, and people. Deviate from the straightness of the stack, and watch gravity take over. Your back is the same. Slouch a little, let time pass, say three or four decades, and watch that slouch get more and more pronounced until you look like that famous Italian tower in Pisa. Yeah, yeah, we know slouching comes from other causes, too, including too little calcium, weak muscles, heredity, and stress.

Take a look at a gaggle of teenagers today, and without having the power of a prophet, you can see their futures—slumped today, back pain tomorrow, pain that might have been avoided through the habit of good posture. It is not too late to make small changes to improve your posture. Why not take a month to give it a try?

Here's the scoop from Larry, who has been teaching about posture (and standing quite straight, thank you very much) for over 30 years.

Slumped shoulders *look* like the culprit that causes bad posture, but the true villains are the lower back, known as the "lumbar region," and its close neighbors, the hips.

**LESSON 1.** To stand straight, your hips need to be aligned directly over your ankles. If your hips are too far forward, the lumbar region curves too much, and you risk strain on the back and surrounding tissue. To make matters worse, your shoulders get in the act by pulling too far back. This misalignment of back, hip, and shoulders creates what we commonly call sway-back—*lordosis* is its medical name.

Back to the hips. If they are too far back, the lumbar curve flattens out. When this occurs, the shoulders compensate by moving out of their alignment—only now they go forward into a slouch. Maintain a slouch for years, and your chest muscles get too short. It's a domino reaction through the body, with the lumbar region and hips leading the way.

Here is more bad news. Over the years, even the slightest misalignment in your posture, whether it is due to swayback, a congenital cause, or slouching, puts excess pressure on your back and surrounding tissue, and considerable strain on your neck. The misalignment can also cause compression to your internal organs, constrict certain blood vessels, and irritate certain nerves, in particular the sciatic nerve that runs down your legs. This can cause excruciating pain, and you may need strong muscle relaxants and pain killers. What to do?

Correcting really bad posture may require a big change, such as surgery, a brace, numerous visits to a chiropractor, or an alternative therapy such as Rolfing. Before such a drastic move, however, consider this small change. Learn to keep your lumbar region in a healthful curve by keeping your shoulders, hips, knees, and ankles stacked on top of each other—in as straight a line as you can attain. How? By practicing *Mountain Pose,* the simple yoga pose we mentioned in the previous section.

**FIRST LESSON.** Stand sideways in front of a mirror. To understand what we are trying to tell you about the relationship between your hips, shoulders, and back, do this demonstration. Stand with your feet together, then slowly rock your hips forward. See where the shoulders and lumbar region go (shoulders back, lumbar curved—too much). Next, rock your hips backward. Shoulders slouch forward, and lumbar loses its curve. Congratulations. You now know how to let gravity get the best of you.

**LESSON 2** is on ankles and feet. Look at yours. Notice how your ankle is directly on top of the front of the *heel*? It is not, please note, over the *ball of your foot.* When you are straight and standing tall, your body weight should be over the front of your heels and not over the ball of your foot. The ball of the foot is for going somewhere, pushing off. The heel is for support, grounding you and giving you balance.

Keeping these two lessons in mind, you are ready to practice Mountain Pose. Remember: shoulders over hips over ankles. Chin parallel to ground, chest expanded but not thrust forward. Feel your lower back in its natural, slightly curved position. Relax your shoulders and be sure they are neither too far forward nor backward. Feel the grounding, the support, the strength of this correct lineup.

Now focus on your breath. With each inhale, imagine your breath lifting you up through the top of your head. With each exhale, relax and enjoy the moment. You are a mountain. You are firm. You are tall. You are serene. Do this every morning, and if you can remember this feeling, it can calm you and give you strength throughout your day.

**WE COULD SUGGEST** other small changes to maintain good posture. For example, we could tell you not to slouch on the sofa while watching TV. We could tell you to sit forward on the seat of your chair in front of your computer. We could tell you to use a special chair with no back and a platform for your knees, a chair that helps your body retain a healthy lumbar curve.

We could tell you to keep a small rolled towel in your car and place it behind your lower back to support your natural curve. We could tell you to use the airplane pillow for lumbar support and see how much better you feel when you disembark. We could tell you that it is best to sleep on your back or your side, and to bend your knees and use your leg muscles when picking up boxes and other objects. We could tell you to switch sides frequently when you carry a shoulder bag or child. We could also tell you to let gravity keep you here on our planet but let proper alignment defend you against gravity's relentless pull. And this: stand tall like a mountain and look better, feel better, and give yourself the best insurance you can against back pain. We could tell you to "stand up straight." But we won't. We trust you know that now.

## Strengthen Your Eye Muscles

Here is a for-what-it-is-worth story. A number of years ago, Susan wrote one of her books sitting in either a local restaurant or in our town's vintage drugstore/ice cream parlor. She thought it would be a change from the writer's usual solitary life.

In these establishments, her coffee cup was continually refilled, so automatically that she failed to notice that she was drinking six to nine cups of coffee a day—enough to give her an ulcer. Along with her new coffee habit, Susan also found herself taking two aspirin to alleviate the headache she always had by dinnertime.

The ulcer brought an end to both her beloved coffee habit and the aspirin. What was she to do instead? She remembered learning some simple eye exercises when we first began doing yoga, back in 1969. Thinking the headaches might have been caused by so much reading and computer work, she thought perhaps the eye exercises would help.

Susan began doing her simple eye exercises—every morning before work, and every afternoon after work. She even added a little yoga to her practice. (Although the yoga didn't last long, it yielded an interesting result, which we will discuss in our section on improving your memory in chapter 4.) When she remembered, she would do a few exercises again before going to sleep. In only a few days the headaches ceased; in a few weeks, she reduced the exercises to once a day. But the story has a twist to it.

A problem arose with her four pairs of eyeglasses (in addition to always misplacing them). She had regular glasses and prescription sunglasses for driving and seeing distances. Then there were reading glasses and even reading sunglasses. None of them seemed right anymore. Everything was blurry. So she went to the eye doctor, who examined her eyes. To her surprise, after the exam, the doctor told her she no longer needed any of the eyewear, as both prescriptions—for nearsightedness and for farsightedness—were too strong.

At first, Susan was skeptical (as you probably are) and considered getting a second opinion. Instead, she gave herself the ultimate test. She loves to sew. Could she thread her needle without glasses? To her surprise, she could—easily. She could read the highway signs without glasses, read books without glasses, and come home from a long day in front of the computer without needing an aspirin. Go figure.

. . .

**HERE ARE THE SIMPLE** eye exercises that may or may not have contributed to Susan's optical success but can strengthen your eye muscles nonetheless. Sit in a comfortable position, back straight, head up (this exercises just your eyes). You may want to take off your glasses or remove your contacts, but it isn't necessary to do so.

**STEP 1.** Up and Down

Point both eyes upward, as high as you can.
Point both eyes downward, as low as you can.
Slowly stretch your eyes up and down two more times. (Told you this was easy.)
Close your eyes for a few seconds.

**STEP 2.** Sideways Left and Right

Point your eyes to the right, as far as you can. (*Note:* your eyes move, not your head.)
Point your eyes to the left, as far as you can.
Slowly stretch your eyes sideways, left and right, two more times.
Close your eyes for a few seconds.

**STEP 3.** Diagonals Back and Forth

Move your eyes up to two o'clock, then down to

seven o'clock, as far as you can stretch them.
Do this three times.

Move your eyes up to eleven o'clock, then down to five o'clock, as far as you can stretch them. Do this three times.

Close your eyes for a few seconds.

**STEP 4.** Round and Round

*Slowly* stretch your eyes by moving around in a clockwise motion three to five times.

Slowly stretch your eyes by moving around in a counterclockwise motion three to five times.

Close your eyes for a few seconds.

**STEP 5.** Rest and Coddle Your Eyes

While your eyes are shut, massage your hands vigorously together until they are warm, then hold them over your eyes for a minute or so.

That's all there is to these simple exercises. We make no promises, although we have read convincing testimonials about similar systems. We do know that exercising your eyes cannot hurt them, will strengthen your eye muscles, will help if you suffer from eye strain, may help relieve headaches, and may even improve your vision.

. . .

**ONE SMALL CHANGE** to make if you work at a computer terminal or read for long stretches is to take more frequent breaks, perhaps in conjunction with the aforementioned eye workouts.

**HERE ARE A** few other small change suggestions related to eyes. Do you rub your eyes without washing your hands first? Not good. Viruses and bacteria can pass through the mucous membranes and threaten your eyes, and the rest of the body as well. One way to break that habit is to give yourself an eye rub whenever you wash your hands. This can reduce your need to rub them at other times and get you accustomed to washing first when the desire to rub overtakes you. This small change can add up to a lifetime of protection for one of your most valuable assets.

And please, please, please stop using spit to clean or moisten your contact lenses. As one does with many habits, you are doing what comes naturally, without thinking about the consequences. (Our friend, Dean, nearly lost his sight because of an infection in one eye caused by that small habit. He is now a reformed spitter, we are happy to report.)

Finally, if you are like Susan's mother and are in the habit of *misplacing* your reading glasses, find a permanent place for them or start attaching them to a neck chain. The five to fifteen minutes you spend searching for them each day could be spent doing something else. Eye exercises, maybe?

## If You Smoke

We know, we know, we know that smoking is out of our league—way out of our league when it comes to giving advice, even though Larry's mother was a longtime smoker who died of a heart attack. Inasmuch as we don't smoke and never have, we called someone who does and asked him to do us a favor and open a cigarette and dump it into a measuring spoon so we could calculate how much tobacco you are likely to smoke in ten years, thirty years, or fifty years.

Our friend said that in his opinion, smoking habits had no place in our book about small change. Now whether he was down to his last cigarette and didn't want to ruin it or whether he is right (that because we don't smoke, we shouldn't be pontificating about small changes you can make as a smoker) is hard to determine, at least as we write this.

Maybe he is correct. If a cancer warning on the package can't stop someone from smoking, what can we say that can? What we do know is this. Smoking is the clearest example of a small habit that takes you *way* off course. If you smoke you probably began as a teenager (and what did you know about smoking then?). If you smoke, you probably began with a few cigarettes and never thought that you would get addicted to them. And if you smoke, you probably aren't seeing each cigarette as one of a *huge* heap of cigarettes, say the 7,300 cigarettes you are likely to smoke *in the next twelve months* (if you smoke only one pack a day), or the 73,000 you are likely to smoke in the next decade. Nor are you seeing the ten thousand dollars or more you will spend buying them during those ten years.

Here is some truly basic information (which you can remind the tobacco industry as well as its lobby groups about, even though it seems obvious that they don't care). Any change you make in smoking—whether it is switching to low-nicotine, low-tar, filtered, or organic cigarettes—short of quitting will mean little in the whole picture of your life. Keep smoking, and you continue to be more likely to develop heart disease, lung disease, cancer, and a face full of wrinkles, and to die several years earlier than you otherwise would. Except that if you cut down from two packs to one pack a day or less, you *might* add a few years to your life expectancy. Or you can look at it the way smokers often look at smoking when they say, "Why worry about the risks . . . ? I could get run over by a truck!" Imagine you are standing on a road and a truck is going to run you over. Does it matter if the truck is ten miles away and going forty-five miles per hour, or if it is five miles away and going fifty miles per hour? The *smartest* thing you can do is to leave the road and avoid getting hit by the truck, thereby making yourself available to some other unknown but hopefully kinder fate.

About all we can suggest is this. Get in the habit of seeing the larger picture and the distant future. By this we mean get in the daily habit of actually *picturing* a scene from your future life. Pretend it is a motion picture or a documentary and look at the people gathered at your funeral who are going to miss you when you die at the age of fifty-nine or sixty-eight instead of at seventy-five or eighty-nine. See a whole generation of grandchildren or even great-grandchildren. See them later, at birthday parties, graduations, and weddings, at holiday dinners, picnics, and vacations—without you.

See the mountain of cigarettes you will not smoke if the next one you smoke is the last one you smoke. Seriously—visualize eating without part of your tongue or jaw, communicating without your voice box, or swallowing after radiation has burned your esophagus. Visualize the stares on the faces of your grandchildren as they see you lug an oxygen tank with you when you accompany them to the mall or the movies. A small change you can make is to visualize one of these consequences *each* and *every* time you light up the first cigarette of the day. Maybe one day one of these visualizations will give you the incentive or courage to quit smoking.

We are proud to say that we ran this section by Max, an outgoing, good-looking, delightful young man, who has smoked since he was thirteen. We never thought he would quit because of anything we said, but we wanted his opinion of the section anyway. Well, Max up and quit that week—because of what he read, he later said. Look, we were as surprised as anyone to know we inspired Max to quit. But if one person quit because of what we wrote, it was worth writing it and worth keeping the section in the book. Worth protecting someone's health and perhaps his or her life. Yeah, it was worth saying. For sure.

## About Those Teeth of Yours

Confession time. Larry flosses regularly, and Susan doesn't, well, floss on a regular basis, and Susan hates, truly hates, going to the dentist. You would think . . .

You would think that every single person reading this book who cares about his or her teeth, who would rather spend four thousand dollars on a vacation than give it to a periodontist, would know the value of flossing and be in the habit of practicing it. You would think. So here's the deal. If you already floss, skip this section, because if you floss regularly, you are probably also using an electric toothbrush and gargling with mouthwash. All we can say is *Congratulations.*

For the rest of you, here is some inspiration. Cavities eventually hurt. Periodontal surgery hurts more, both in your mouth and in your pocket. Losing teeth hurts, too, socially and psychologically. Flossing is the best habit you can cultivate to prevent all that misfortune.

**RULE 1.** Floss only around the teeth you want to keep.

**RULE 2.** Floss every day. Plaque begins to form in only

twenty-four hours, so everyday flossing is best for removing food and plaque, as well as for exercising gum tissue.

Larry travels frequently to foreign places. Rather than floss and risk infecting his gums with a local germ, our dentist advised him to get in the habit of using mouthwash after brushing. Although it falls short of flossing, it *is* effective in killing many germs that form plaque and better than doing nothing at all. Which leads us to . . .

**RULE 2 MODIFIED.** If flossing *every* day is too big a change, consider an everyday mouthwash *plus* two to three flossings per week. Clearly, this does not compete with daily flossing for good dental hygiene, but it will both reduce the dental plaque and exercise the gums. The shift to daily flossing can be another small change in the future.

Then there is the issue of brushing your teeth. It is best to brush at night before going to bed (the time that brushing gives you the most protection against bacteria and decay), so if you have fallen out of that habit, it is clearly a good one to reinstate. Another small change is to start brushing your tongue, which reduces germs and refreshes your entire mouth. Still another small though really important change is to avoid the habit of sharing toothbrushes—a very bad idea.

As for electric toothbrushes, do not regard them as a substitute for flossing—they are not. They do make brushing easier and more fun. And they do stimulate the gums, but so does brushing, if you are conscientious. At any rate, our dentist and hygienist report a big difference between those who use one and those who don't. (Larry uses one, Susan doesn't. For her birthday one year, Larry gave Susan an electric toothbrush. She cried. It's not that it wasn't a personal gift. What could be more personal than your toothbrush? Maybe it was just *too* practical.)

**NOW FOR SOME** bad habits you might consider breaking. *Stop chewing ice.* It is one of the easiest ways to crack a tooth. If you can't stop chewing ice, then start ordering your drinks without it. Avoiding temptation is a lot easier than exercising self-control, as any ice chewer knows.

If you have a tendency to put off going to the dentist, *get in the habit of making regular appointments,* preferably every six months, more often if your teeth build up a lot of plaque.

**PERHAPS THE BEST WAY** to inspire yourself to acquire good dental habits is to add up the benefits—a better smile, sweeter breath, and in the future, less pain, fewer hassles, and a ton of money you can put in *your* savings account instead of your dentist's savings account.

And if you have those recurring dreams about your teeth, where they are loose or falling out, don't take the dream literally. According to some dream experts, loose teeth mean that you are feeling a loss of control or a change in your life. But maybe, just maybe, it is a cosmic sign that the next small change you should consider is to improve your dental health.

## Wash Your Hands and Blow Your Nose

Look, as crime goes, not washing your hands is not the *worst* thing in the world. Besides, consider this dirty little secret. Although most people *say* they wash their hands after using the restroom, only about one out of three really do.

Getting into the habit of washing your hands, at least three times a day, is a very good thing. It is the *single most important means of preventing the spread of infection.* This is worth repeating. Washing your hands is the single most important means of preventing the spread of infection.

Washing your hands as few as three times a day can reduce your chance of getting a common cold or flu and other infectious diseases by at least forty percent. Consider this payoff, too. The average cold takes five days to get over, fourteen to twenty-eight days if you develop complications like bronchitis or persistent coughing. So let's do some estimates for *one* illness:

5 days (if you are lucky): 7,200 minutes of sickness and discomfort
14 days (complications): 20,160 minutes
28 days (those damn germs): 40,360 minutes

Sparing yourself the misery and inconvenience of one short illness, by spending a mere three minutes a day washing your hands, takes approximately 1,000 minutes a year. Check the math. It looks like a no-brainer to us. You might even avoid more than one illness or a really serious infection, such as SARS. Most important to remember: washing your hands is easy, being sick is not.

Need to wash your hands quite frequently? Don't always have access to soap and water? A great alternative to handwashing is a hand sanitizer made of an alcohol gel lotion. Gel lotion cannot scrub away the dirt, but it is an effective germ killer. And what's great about gels is the time you can save—they take only seconds to use. According to one study of health-care workers, gel users saved up to an hour on a ten-hour shift. Now that's a small change that adds up over time.

ANNIE MAE, the friend of ours who often shares her wisdom with us, taught us to wash our fruits and vegetables, not just because of the pesticides, which is one important reason, but because of all those people she sees touching fruits and vegetables as they shop and perhaps passing on infections. Well, that's Annie Mae's theory, and she's a pretty healthy person; thus we respect it. So get out of the habit of eating grapes, apples, pears, peaches, or tomatoes before washing them.

AT THE RISK of grossing you out, especially if you are reading this book as you eat, we (Larry, really) want to talk about mucus. Yup (he insisted).

Mucus, according to Larry's basic, never-took-biology-in-college-but-think-I-know-something-about-it-because-I-have-taught-yoga-for-over-thirty-years understanding is that mucus is the body's trap for germs and viruses and other harmful invaders. He says it is the town jail—compared to the state prison. (HUH? Whatever!) That's because it is a temporary holding cell and not long-term incarceration.

Since we are publishing his theory, we thought it best to find research to back it up. Amazingly, Larry was right. Besides lubricating the body and protecting its tissues, mucus *is* one of the body's cleaning systems, especially for the lungs and intestinal tract. Here's the scoop. Mucus collects and holds in suspension the body's invaders, such as pollen, certain germs, and other stuff, until it can be discharged. So, for your possible small change—should you choose to make this your next small change—get out of the habit of swallowing your mucus and into the habit of blowing your nose. (Not blowing into your napkin, however, which we already discussed, but blowing into a tissue.) Out of the body and onto something else. Could not be simpler—except perhaps remembering to do it. And remembering not to discuss this one at the dinner table when you talk about your small change for the month.

## Are You Sleepy?

If you are often sleepy, we have some terrific small changes for you to try, especially if you have been relying on coffee or complaining to get you through the day.

First, though, take this little true or false test:

T/F ________ I need an alarm to wake up in the morning. (Or someone who *acts* like an alarm, such as my companion telling me I'm late for work, my children scurrying in the room, or my dog nudging me to get up and let him out.)

T/F ________ I need a cup of coffee to energize myself.

T/F ________ I am so tired in the afternoon that I *want,* but do not, of course, allow myself, to be cranky with others, including, on occasion, myself.

T/F ________ As soon as my head hits the pillow I fall asleep (normally, it should take 10 to 20 minutes before you fall asleep).

**SCORE:** If you answer *true* to *any* of these questions, there is an excellent chance that you are getting less sleep than you actually require to be a functional, pleasant, and productive human being. Nor are you alone—half of the people in the industrial world share your plight.

If you always find yourself too sleepy or too tired to do what you want or need to do, the best small change you can make for yourself may be to make an appointment for a physical checkup to rule out a medical condition. If there is no medical condition, then the best change you can make is to go to sleep earlier. This means you need to *start getting to bed earlier.* You may be in the habit of underestimating how much time it takes to get ready for going to sleep. As Larry likes to say, "Tomorrow always starts the night before."

Sometimes getting to sleep earlier, sleeping through the night, or sleeping later is beyond your control. For those times, we have suggestions that may help you feel better. Here they are.

*Get in the habit of taking a power nap.* Learn to take a power nap, ten to twenty minutes long, to feel refreshed for the next four to six hours.

*Do a "really rest."* For five to ten minutes, sit quietly, perhaps closing your eyes and breathing slowly, or thinking pleasant and relaxing thoughts—about things like being at the beach or watching a sunset. If you can, tense a few muscles, especially your facial muscles; then release the tension. Or give yourself a minimassage (on your neck, head, shoulders, or feet). Or convince your office manager to let a massage therapist come in at lunch or the end of the day and give people a ten- to fifteen-minute shoulder massage.

*Have a healthy snack.* Not a sugar or carbohydrate one, which will give you an energy boost but then shortly afterward lower your blood sugar and make you feel worse than before. (Reread the earlier section on snacking for more suggestions, such as a handful of nuts or seeds, peanut butter on crackers, a glass of milk, a container of yogurt, or a slice of cheese or turkey.)

*Meditate.* Ten minutes of meditation equals about one hour of sleep; twenty minutes equals about two hours of sleep. And meditation doesn't leave you with that sluggish feeling that a long nap often does. (Jump ahead to page 175 for instructions on meditation.)

*Get fresh air.* Open the windows or go outside for five minutes. A blast of fresh air can do wonders.

*Splash cold water on your face.*

*Do as the English do.* Instead of your afternoon coffee break, indulge in teatime (where you brew the tea, eat little sandwiches or cheese balls, and fully comprehend the meaning of leisure).

*Change your shoes.* This is a small change Susan stumbled upon one year during her endless search for stylish but extremely comfortable shoes. She found that changing her shoes, especially after standing or walking all day, rejuvenated her almost instantly. In fact, to avoid unnecessary fatigue, get in the habit of wearing *truly* comfortable shoes throughout the day.

*Eat well.* Get in the habit of eating a healthful breakfast if you want to be in the habit of feeling good in the afternoon.

**IF YOU MAKE** any or all of these changes and are still tired all the time, perhaps you have a bigger problem. You may have a medical condition that requires treatment.

You may need a new mattress, a different pillow, earplugs, or a change in your job, your household, your life.

Here is the bottom line. If you keep doing what you have always been doing, you will keep getting the same results. Take small steps toward improving your sleep, and you may find that your waking life improves—in a big way.

# 3. Small Changes for Better Relationships

We thrive on good relationships. The quality of our relationships, in fact, helps to define who we are and how we live our lives, what is important to us and what is not, how successfully we find love and how well we overcome adversity, what is our purpose in living and how we connect to all living beings.

Small change has the power to vastly improve all our relationships. It is not, however, a program for achieving perfection. Nor should it become a platform for changing others. (Remember, small change is about *your* self-improvement, not someone else's.)

Small change is an easy way to improve your relationships, since they depend so much on the little details. Almost as soon as you make a change, you will notice an improvement. Make small change a constant, and those improvements will add up over time—one of the surest ways to increase your happiness in life.

## Make Friends with Yourself

And now for the Terkel Theory of Everlasting Love. *Make friends with yourself.* This theory may strike you as too obvious to state, as having little to do with small change and much more to do with needing fifteen years of intense, daily psychotherapy. But hear us out. We are not saying that you *have* to like yourself, although that is a great idea. What we are saying is that to enjoy a good relationship with yourself, you need to accept who you are and learn to get along with yourself, much the way you would need to get along with a conjoined twin. And when you mess up, you need to learn how to forgive yourself so that you can continue to live peacefully with yourself.

The following suggestions may sound hokey—but do them anyway. They can improve the most important relationship in your life.

*Start each day with a smile.* Smile at the person you see in the mirror. (See page 228 for more on the benefits of smiling.)

*When you can't find something nice to say about yourself, don't say anything at all.* The next time—in fact, every time—you find yourself putting yourself down, stop midsentence and change the subject. (When others put themselves down, we always stop them midsentence and give them an opportunity to "take back what they just said"—a rule Susan uses in her writing workshops.)

*Indulge yourself.* Take a few hours (and when you can, an entire day or evening) to indulge yourself in something . . . well, indulgent. Treat yourself to a long bath, take a walk, go to an art museum, listen to an opera from beginning to end. The goal here is to enjoy your own company—alone. If you are uneasy spending time alone, activities such as these will slowly make a powerful shift: from seeing yourself as lonely to enjoying yourself—alone.

*Talk to yourself.* Give yourself a time each day, for example when going on a walk by yourself, to engage in an inner dialogue with yourself.

*Treat yourself as you would your best friend.* Learn to get along with yourself as you would get along with a *best* friend. Improve yourself, which is what we have been saying all along, but don't expect to transform into someone new or someone you are not. You wouldn't expect that of a best friend, so why expect that of yourself? Allow yourself faults, as you do in a friend.

*Be thoughtful.* If "you" like a clean room, make the bed and pick things up—for you. If "you" like soft music, put on the soft music. If "you" would rather shop than exercise, or read than clean, stop worrying about what you ought to be doing and do what your "self" wants to do—not always, perhaps, but at least sometimes.

Here are some other small changes for balancing this area of your life.

*Build yourself up.* Give yourself credit for what you do well and what makes you special. If you are in the habit of tooting your own horn, also referred to as bragging, however, remember the saying that nobody likes a braggart.

*Keep a junk drawer of bad habits.* Yes, this book is about

self-improvement. Yes, bad habits take you off course. Remember, though, that this is about self-improvement, not total transformation. So if you are accustomed to working too hard on self-improvement, here's a useful small change: List five to ten bad habits. Pick two to three. These are yours to keep forever, *if you like.* (Note, we didn't say the entire list, just a few.) Now here is the caveat. Temper these faults. If you are hotheaded, for example, don't give it up; just vow to be *less* angry or angry less of the time. If you are stubborn, try to be less stubborn or stubborn less of the time. If you are a slob, learn to confine it to fewer rooms in the house. You will still be you—just a modified and improved version.

Like all small changes that add up, treating yourself as you would treat others will add up to a lifetime of less stress, less guilt, and more pleasure. Or, as we say, a lifetime of everlasting love.

## My Way or Your Way?

Are you the hot sauce in a relationship? We're talking General Tso's chicken or pad Thai noodles. Too heavy on the hot chile peppers, and all you taste is fire. Relationships are the same. Go heavy on hot ingredients such as anger, stubbornness, or self-righteousness, and what you get is fire—and you'll need to devote an awful lot of energy putting it out. Metaphors aside, when you cool the habits that erode a relationship, you improve your whole life.

Number one on our list of hot buttons is temper. Improve the short-circuit on a temper, and you will have fewer arguments, less stress, better health, and improved relationships. One way to cool a temper is the tried-and-true method of counting to ten when you feel it heating up. Another is to get control of your breathing. Still another is to focus your mind on something else like shooting baskets, going for a run, or playing the guitar.

Are you in the habit of playing "devil's advocate" and always taking the opposite point of view—no matter what you really think? Since this habit irritates and annoys so many people, having it puts you at risk of irritating and annoying many people. Why not save the devil's advocate for the classroom and employ more agreeable social skills?

Another habit that undermines relationships is always wanting to be right or needing to get your way. Being open-minded and open to seeing another viewpoint allows you to deepen your understanding of a situation. Wouldn't it be nice if others found you more tolerant, less judgmental, and less rigid? The easiest way to be open-minded with others is to ask them what they think and feel, then patiently (and nondefensively), *carefully listen to them explain* themselves. (See page 99.)

Still another socially useful small change is to be mindful of the tone of your voice or your stance when you disagree with someone else. The tendency to raise your voice, for example, can immediately put others on the defensive and make them unable or unwilling to hear you out. Combative stances and other aggressive body language—from hands on hips and finger-pointing to scowls and grimaces—can also work against a relationship. And let's be candid, if you are earnest about improving your relationships, get out of the habit of cursing at other people.

Want to cut down on nagging, criticism, and arguments? Try this small change in your home and place of work. Install a suggestion box, with the rule that in order for a suggestion to be considered by you, suggestions have to be in printable language and be honest, sincere, and tactful.

**NO ONE *LIKES*** to lose an argument or be in the doghouse, but life guarantees times when this occurs. We recognize that big transgressions require big changes and are therefore outside the scope of this book.

Nonetheless, being in the habit of apologizing sincerely *and completely* for small conflicts in life prepares you to apologize for serious wrongdoings and misdeeds in the future.

To improve the actual way you apologize, allow yourself to be less defensive and more honestly remorseful when you apologize. This requires a little humility, as well as being better at empathizing with the other person's perspective (trying harder to see it in the first place, for example).

We suggest the following three-act drama—in this case, it is a documentary drama, since sincerity and truthfulness are requisite.

**ACT 1 (THE REMORSE):** "I'm sorry."

**ACT 2 (THE EXPLANATION):** "Because . . ."

**ACT 3 (JUSTICE):** "This is what I'll do to make amends." (You can't always mend a broken dish or right a wrong, but you can always make an earnest attempt to try.)

A little advice for act 2: explain, don't excuse, yourself. Giving excuses may dilute your apology, as it indicates an unwillingness to accept blame. If you don't understand the distinction, give it some thought, because it is an important issue.

To improve the way you *accept* an apology, we offer these suggestions.

*Put a statute of limitations on the length of time you hold a grudge or hold on to bad feelings.* Our statute of limitations is as follows. Up to a few hours for small spats over punctuality or issues that will soon be forgotten; a day or so for repeat offenses; and no more than a few years for serious transgressions (unless you want to end a relationship, and then it is not a small matter, and small change may not be able to help you mend the relationship).

*Get in the habit of giving people second chances.* To err is human, as the saying goes. Cultivating the habit of giving people a second chance when they screw up will give you a lifetime of stronger relationships. (Note, however, that we said "second," not fifth, tenth, or twentieth chance). This is a small change that can add up to a *very* big dividend in life. We repeat, a very big dividend.

**HERE ARE A FEW** more suggestions to help you improve your relationships with others.

*Go on a low-criticism (as in low-cal) diet.* Cut the amount of criticism you dish out by half. Ditto for unsolicited advice, which is often a subtle form of criticism.

*Eliminate "never" and "always" from your fighting vocab-*

*ulary,* as in "You never (fill in the blank)" or "You always (fill in the blank)." These two words are surefire obstacles to moving forward in a relationship because they lock out optimism and make it more difficult for the other person to want to change. Besides, they are usually exaggerations and therefore not the truth anyway.

**IF YOU ARE** in the habit of doing whatever it takes to get your way, *ease up*. Or, in the common vernacular, lighten up. If you are in the habit of seeing relationships as power struggles or competitions, where there is always a winner and a loser (and you struggle hard not to be the loser), then again, lighten up and learn to find more common ground. And finally, look for ways to ensure that the heat from your relationships comes from the excitement of being in them and not from the friction that can destroy them.

## Phone Home

Confession time. At the end of college vacations, we each had to drive several hours to get to our college in upstate New York. We would call our parents collect and give the operator a designated name that signaled our parents that we were the callers. Susan would give the name Jasmine—the name of her family pet. Her parents could accept or refuse to accept the call but were reassured that Susan had arrived safely. (Okay, we are not proud to have been dishonest about this, but it was not all that difficult to rationalize.)

Phoning home has always been an important way to stay connected to the people you love. Have you let the habit slip of calling home, either to your parents, spouse, companion, or children? Why not get back into the habit? These calls don't have to be long—nor do they need any more content than to say *I was thinking about you.*

If you let weeks go by without calling home or without reaching someone at home, try to revive the old-fashioned custom of Sunday evening phone calls (we used to call home then because the rates were the cheapest). If you have an elderly parent, try getting into the habit of a short phone call every day or every other day—just to check in, just to say *I love you.*

And speaking of affection, if you do care about the person, get into the habit of ending the phone call by telling them how much they mean to you. This can add hundreds, even thousands, of endearments to your relationship over the years, because such endearments *do* add up.

On the subject of endearments, think about how often you say "I love you"—or don't say it. Some people dole out *I love you*s stingily, in the misguided belief that if you don't hear it very often, it will retain more of its meaning. We don't buy that one. Saying *I love you*—when you mean it—is probably one of the most powerful things you can say to someone—because the minute you don't love them, it is the hardest thing to say.

Take a few minutes and think about your habits—the habit of calling home on a regular basis, the habit of telling loved ones how much they mean to you. And if you are too busy to remember to call, then you are too, too busy. And if you are that busy, you probably won't take our advice, or make this small change. But everyone would win if you tried.

## The Standing Date

Personally, we hate the expression *quality time* for the way it implies that the rest of the time you spend with someone, is, well, not so great. We prefer to call quality time *the standing date*—a time you spend focused on the person with whom you have the most valuable relationship in your life. (*Note:* It is not the *only* valuable relationship.) If you are living with a lover or spouse, this is the person. It could also be your best friend, a parent, a child, or a sibling. The point here is that you are going to get in the habit of having a standing date with whomever holds first place in your inner circle of relationships—or with whomever *should* be in first place.

All good relationships need time when the two people can screen out the noise of the world and concentrate on each other. The standing date, which occurs at least once a week, is especially important for people caught up in superbusy careers or for parents of newborns and young children. Young parents need to get in the habit of eating at least one meal together sans the little ones. Can't afford a sitter? Then trade off your children with another couple (cousins are a great choice). Or join a babysitting cooperative. (By the way, offering your babysitting services is a great present for a young couple—you might consider giving them a standing date coupon book.)

*One and a half hours a week equals seventy-eight hours of focused time a year, the equivalent of a five- to seven-day vacation with someone when you subtract sleeping.*

When our children were young, we preferred that our standing date be at a restaurant. We chose restaurants with booths because they gave us more privacy and somehow seemed more cozy, relaxing places. Budget constraints? Choose a walk in the park or the woods, or coffee at a local diner. Or meet European-style for a drink before dinner. What is important is to choose a place that ensures you time for talking with minimal distractions and interruptions.

Splurge and celebrate an anniversary or promotion or anything else special somewhere else. For your standing date it helps to choose a place within your budget so you won't be tempted to cancel the standing date when funds run low. And if you make your standing date at the same place each week, its familiarity can help the two of you spend less time studying the menu and more time focused on each other. If you prefer variety, then rotate between two or three places.

A few rules help out here. One rule is to try your best, your *very* best, to avoid using this time to settle differences or work out problems. Rather, treat the time as if you were on a "date." Stay on the positive side. You can have a lively discussion, but try to avoid criticizing. (Practice "biting your tongue"! A good habit to cultivate anyway.)

The beauty of the standing date is how easy it becomes to plan the rest of the week around it. The only time we broke a standing date was for a sick child. If you have a busy schedule and find it difficult to make a standing date or if you are separated by physical distance, then make your standing date a time when you can relax and enjoy a long, uninterrupted telephone conversation. Our point is that if your life is too busy to set aside a standing date, then it is too busy. And if you get in the habit of a standing date, you will be in the habit of making the most important person in your life feel—important!

## Keep the Connection Strong

Want to guarantee that enough people show up at your funeral? (*That* got your attention!) Honestly, do you want to go through life enjoying the company of good friends and great family? To have a strong cheering squad, and people who want to see you succeed? To have people who will share your birthdays, graduations, weddings, job promotions, and other milestones? Do you want people in your life with whom you can share happiness, sorrow (unless, of course, they are the *cause* of it!), and everything in between? Consider this. Small changes you make to strengthen the relationships with your family and close friends can add up over your entire life.

One self-improvement may be to focus more attention on the relationships that matter the most to you. One way to do this is by setting aside a regular time during your week or during the month to make contact with them. This can be a regular time to catch up on your correspondence, make phone calls, or actually spend time with family or friends who you care about but don't often get to see. Larry, for example, periodically sets a date and makes plans to meet his brother and sister for lunch or dinner. Once a week Susan writes or calls one or two people who live far away because she values her relationship with them.

Another idea is to spend a month organizing a reunion of old friends. Our friend Karen celebrated a milestone birthday by organizing a reunion with her high school girlfriends. Or you could plan a family reunion, as our friend Molly does each summer. She and her five grown children and all their children pitch in to rent a summer cottage (a big one, of course, but nothing fancy). Same week each summer. Another family friend, Joe, goes camping every *other* year with his parents, five siblings, and all their spouses and children.

Still another idea is to use the month to assemble a date book of birthdays, anniversaries, and addresses and get in the habit of checking it at the beginning or end of each month. Add a stack of blank or assorted greeting cards, stamps, and a few gift catalogs, and thoughtfulness becomes easier than ever.

**WANT TO GIVE** a gift to an elderly family member and get a priceless gift in return? Each time you visit a parent, grandparent, or other member of the family, bring along a notebook, recorder, or video camera and get in the habit of taking a half hour or so to record their stories and wisdom for posterity. Someday that documentation will be one of your family treasures. For Susan, it was the beginning of her writing career.

**LEST YOU THINK** we have a perfect grip on family and friends, think again. We don't. (No one does.) From our experience, however, we know this. Nothing erodes or destroys a family or friendship faster or more completely than a small misunderstanding or wrongdoing left to fester. While time may heal, the passage of time also allows distance to grow. One of the best (though not easiest) habits, therefore, is not to wait when you think something is wrong, no matter how trivial the cause of the trouble. The alternative would be to "grant" the other party a reprieve for a small misunderstanding or wrongdoing, especially if it is out of character for that person. Either habit allows you to maintain a healthy perspective—and, hopefully, maintain the quality of the relationship.

We have also learned this from experience (with two weddings). Until you have had a few weddings or other expensive affairs to plan, let go of feeling hurt if you or your children are not invited. The guest list is *always* complicated, and it is *always* difficult to please everyone on or off it, especially if the budget is limited.

If you often wish you had a better family or circle of friends, you could try small changes to improve your tolerance of these people in your life. First, when a family member or friend is embarrassing, let it embarrass *them,* not you. (This requires loving detachment.) Perceiving them as characters in a successful sitcom might help you become more tolerant, gain a healthier perspective, and sharpen your sense of humor. After all, this is where writers and comics mine some of their best material.

On the other hand, when family or friends are abusive, when they threaten your emotional or physical well-being, or safety, divorce them. (Seriously. Although this is a big change, and we are not discussing big changes.)

**REMEMBER THAT** a small change is an improvement you make on yourself, not one you impose on others. When the people closely connected to you don't share your values, when they fail to reciprocate your hospitality and overtures, it is okay if you decide not to put yourself out for people who don't put themselves out for you. You are allowed to be human, after all. Often, though, staying connected *is* a lopsided affair, with one person or family member making more of an effort than the other. The time spent together, however, can still result in a good relationship. Perhaps the example you set will help the other party eventually come around. In the meantime, you have the satisfaction of making the effort and taking the high road.

By staying in touch with people you love, remembering important dates, sharing both happy and sad times, and being as tolerant as possible, you strengthen the relationships that mean the most. With each connection, strong relationships grow stronger.

## The Secret to Showing You Care

Have we got a gem for you—a tiny three-letter word that is easy to overlook yet describes one of the most powerful ways you can show you care about someone else. This word is the secret to making a good first impression and the secret to maintaining close relationships. It adds spark to casual encounters and deepens intimate interludes.

What do we think is one of the most useful words in the entire lexicon? *Ask.* Yes, ask.

The reason *ask* is so powerful is that to ask is to connect, to show how much you respect the other person, to show that you care. This doesn't have to be a deep connection—this can be as brief as, "Are you having a good day?" Or "How are you today?" But when you really mean it they will take notice.

With more time, you can ask someone about their work, their families, their interests, their opinions, their role models, their favorite sections of the newspaper, books, stories, movies, songs, and childhood memories. When you ask and when you listen to their answers, your actions are speaking even louder than your words. They are expressing your respect, your care, your concern for what they have to say.

Asking is also how we learn. It helps you to put yourself in someone else's shoes, helps you see their viewpoint, helps you discover what is unique about them, and helps you get beyond what might have been a misleading first impression.

**WE WOULD LIKE** to give you the benefit of the doubt and assume that you know what *not* to ask, what questions are too personal, too sensitive, or none of your business. If you remain clueless here are a few samples: "Are you pregnant?" (Wait to be told. Asking someone who isn't is the equivalent of a centipede putting all its feet in its mouth.) "How much did that cost?" "How much do you earn?"

Often what is permissible or taboo is dictated by culture. Americans, for example, generally tolerate and even welcome questions about what they do for a living, while in Europe, the query is often considered intrusive. If you are mindful of personal boundaries, you will not risk offending others or putting yourself in a bad light.

Remember that good conversation is not a monologue (you doing all the talking or the other person doing all the talking) but a give and take. Aim for balance, aspire for interesting. Don't expect small talk and casual conversation to reach the heights of a senior seminar in philosophy. If you rely on the word *ask,* you will always be able to keep the conversation going—or have a reasonable excuse to get going.

Talking about themselves is usually everyone's favorite topic. As a good audience who provides thoughtful questions, you endear yourself to them, but if a person never asks you a question in return, you might find a reasonable excuse to move on to someone else's interesting stories. They are not showing much sensitivity to you, and you don't have to be a martyr, after all.

If this advice rings true to you for casual encounters, it can be even more important in your close relationships. Friends may be there to share your problems, but not all the time. They want you to care about their life as well. Get in the habit of asking, and you won't have to wonder why they are always so busy when you call.

Finally, there are your most significant relationships. When you stop asking questions, when you assume you know what the other person has to say, you risk having them feel that you are taking them for granted. If you want to keep passion alive, if you want to keep relationships fresh, keep asking and keep caring.

Making this small change in how you approach people will deepen your connection to them. It works in both directions—you connect with others and you help others connect with you.

Asking questions and being genuinely interested in the answers is a secret that can make a big difference in every relationship in your life, every single one.

## The Terkel Take on Talking

Speaking of the all-important asking, good communication in general is the gold standard for all good relationships. Improving your skill at both listening and talking will improve nearly all your relationships, from casual acquaintances to close bonds. In this section there are enough habits to change for anyone to find something to work on—including us. (Larry was the inspiration for this section, and Susan talked too much about it.)

First, though, may we remind you of the best habit of all, which one conversation pundit called the Golden Rule of Listening. *Listen as you would have others listen to you.* To which we add: *Speak as you would have others speak about you.* (In other words, refrain from spreading rumors and character assaults.)

Sketches follow of some less-than-appealing conversation styles. For each, mindfulness would be the key to making small changes. (If all the descriptions fit you, may we suggest signing up for a course at charm school. You may need the extra communication skills they can help you develop.)

**THE PROSECUTOR.** Are you in the habit of arguing and challenging *every single* statement a person makes? Ordinary conversations are not courtrooms, so why put people on the defensive all the time?

**THE FACT CHECKER.** Do you frequently interrupt a conversation to correct the facts? This often occurs when someone close to you is telling other people a story you know well. Not to break your bubble, but we believe it is our duty to let you know that the narrator of the *Odyssey* probably took artistic liberties with the story. Most stories just don't have to be told *exactly* as they occurred—especially not ones for the sake of entertainment or enlightenment. If the storyteller is your companion, spouse, parent, or child, you could improve your relationship (and everyone else's pleasure) by keeping your mouth shut and your tongue tied.

**THE STORY STEALER.** Someone, usually your partner or parent, starts telling a story. Because you think you tell it better, or have the right to tell it (or because you aren't thinking), you butt in and take over. This is known as stealing. And darling, this is a very bad habit.

Here's some advice for story stealers. If you want to be orthodox about this (instead of being mellow), follow this guideline. For stories you share, it's first come, first serve. For stories that ought to be yours (because they happened to you), tough it out. (You are a grown-up now, and besides, other people don't want to listen to you battle out ownership of a story, for Pete's sake.) Better yet, break the habit of stealing stories, and others may gift you with the habit of letting you finish them.

***I-top-you* and *I-have-one-just-like-the-one-you-told.*** After listening to someone's story, you tell one that either "tops" theirs or is similar enough to express solidarity with the one they told. Nice intentions, but consider this. *Usually one story on a particular topic is enough.* If their story is great, telling one of your own, especially if it is going to be better, steals their thunder. Our advice: give it up.

**THE EPIC NARRATOR.** Before you begin recounting an epic, be sure your listener is up to the task of hearing one. And be sure, too, that you aren't telling an epic when a short story will suffice.

**THE WALL.** This is someone who tries (earnestly sometimes) to act as if he or she is listening but is actually making out a to-do list or is concentrating on the speaker's mole, oversized diamond ring, or nonessential but rarely overlooked body parts. Honey, if you are a wall, you ain't foolin' nobody.

**HOW EASY IT IS** to dispense advice; how difficult to follow one's own advice. We may be hypocrites here; we admit it. We have some bad, bad habits and will work on them in the future, though only one at a time.

Here are more conversation corrupters.

**THE SWIFT CHANGER.** Swift changers move to a new topic so quickly, they don't leave enough time to wrap up the first topic. Polite people may try to effect a swift change with an "Oh, by the way," but this doesn't alter the situation. If you are a swift changer, you may want to practice curbing your impulse to speed up a conversation, because other people may wonder if you are truly listening to them or care about what they just said or if you suffer from a severe case of mind roving.

**THE TALKER-OVER.** In our family, we acquired the custom of what our daughter-in-law Alicia calls "talking-over." It is a conversational skill that requires much practice (not just anyone can pull it off—it takes two to tango, so to speak), and, like steak tartare or oysters, is not appreciated by all. Here goes. Just as some people can do more than one thing at a time, Susan (who learned this from her college roommate, Kim) and our son Ari can talk and listen to each other *at the same time. Talking over has to be mutual,* or else you risk the other person feeling as if you think that what they think is not as important as what you think.

**THE HEAVY FOOT.** As the other person is talking, you

step in and start talking, too. Unlike talking over, though, you have stopped listening to what they say, perhaps because you don't care what they are saying (or shouting, as is often the case). This is ineffective communication and, like cutting off a car on the road, can lead to a dangerous outcome. Give it up and you will be richly rewarded.

**THE INTERRUPTER.** We are a mixed marriage here. Larry doesn't interrupt anyone and doesn't like being interrupted (although he is long-winded), while Susan interrupts but also doesn't mind being interrupted (because she runs on at the mouth and knows it). Refraining from interrupting *is* a worthy habit to acquire, especially if you are a therapist, but it doesn't have to be an absolute rule. The key to acceptable interrupting is to remember to say "excuse me," *and* to do it sparingly. It *is* an effective technique with people who monopolize a conversation or are so excited they don't let you get a word in edgewise.

We are willing, however, to cut enthusiastic conversationalists some slack. While it is true that people who interrupt are showing a lack of consideration, they may have extremely quick minds or tremendous enthusiasm for the topic of conversation. If we are ranking people by the seriousness of their character flaws, Interrupters (like people who chew with their mouths open) are not the worst people in the world, despite what your therapist says about them.

**THE MONOPOLIZER.** First, here's an old but reliable rule. Since you have two ears and one mouth, you should listen twice as much as you talk. Do you monopolize conversations? Worse, do you pontificate and throw your knowledge around as though your words are sacred? (Yeah, yeah, we know we are being tough here.) This is our advice. If you want to lecture, get a soapbox and go to the park, or sign up with a speaker's bureau and get paid. Become a member of the clergy, a professor, or president of an organization. When you are engaged in light social banter, however, stop hogging the air time, *no matter who you are, how charming you may be, or the value of what you think you have to say.* If you have this tendency (and we think you know who you are), you might try glancing at your watch to let yourself know when your talking time ought to be up.

**THE TEASER.** Have you outgrown teasing yet? If not, grow up. Get in the habit of reflecting on whether your humor is appropriate for the social setting before you tell jokes at another person's expense, speak crudely, or poke fun at someone. Some people (such as Susan, she wants to tell you) are too sensitive to take ribbing or practical jokes, so why risk hurting them?

**THE GRAMMAR GUARDIAN AND THE PUNSTER.** Are you in the habit of correcting people's grammar when they are talking to you? Or making puns of what they say? Both interrupt an otherwise intelligent or thoughtful conversation, so do this sparingly—or not at all.

**THE JARGONEER.** On the list of thou-shalt-nots, this one is low. Still, it might be a small change you want to make to improve your relationships with those you encounter. Try to avoid using professional jargon or acronyms with people who are not in your profession or field of interest.

If you are one of those rare few who don't have a single bad conversational habit, then you can spend your next small change practicing other communication skills. Our son Dave, for example, practiced lifting one eyebrow. Now he can communicate more with that lift than most people can say in three minutes of talking.

You may think we have made enough suggestions to last your lifetime and given a disproportionate amount of attention to the topic. How we speak and how we listen, though, are one of the most essential ways we form relationships with other people. Hey, can you top that?!

## The Ultimate Gift

Looking for the perfect gift? With the potential to last an *entire lifetime*? A gift that can bring immeasurable joy, self-esteem, and pride? Something that brings as much joy to the giver as the receiver? A gift to treasure?

How about a plain old compliment? (First of all, it will cost you nothing!)

Getting into the habit of paying compliments gets you in the habit of seeing people in a good light—and in the habit of acknowledging what is good about them. Try just telling people what you like about them, or put it in the form of a thank-you note: "Thanks for that joke. You can see the humor in anything. I love being with such a witty person." Or it can be as simple as: "Nice job."

Some people think that if they pay too many compliments, they risk appearing fawning or insincere. This is where the honesty part of our formula comes in. Honest compliments are never fawning—they are simply honest compliments. Isn't it better to risk appearing too complimentary than risk being stingy with your compliments? Haven't you heard people bemoan the fact that their parents never complimented them when they deserved it? ("Why didn't you get an A instead of only a B?" "Too bad you couldn't get another hit and win the game.")

Another reason for honesty is that compliments that are given without being earned may later spoil a person's full pleasure in a deserved compliment. For example, praising everything a child does—calling every picture or poem wonderful, for example—gives the child a false sense that everything they do is praiseworthy, and this is not true. On the other hand, missing an opportunity to praise work that is truly outstanding or that took a great effort diminishes the excitement a person deserves to enjoy.

One caveat here. Reassurance differs from a compliment and can stretch the truth a bit, in our opinion. Reassurance that something is "fine, just fine," is different from "Wow! That's great." Sometimes all we need to hear is that we are okay—we don't need accolades to be reassured.

**NOW, MANY PEOPLE** who would gladly accept an expensive gift from you may show reluctance to accept your free compliment. (And if you are one of these people, then listen up.) All an honest compliment deserves is a smile and a thank-you. It does not require a personal put-down—"Oh, this old dress?" Or an explanation—"Well, to tell you the truth, it isn't my dress. I borrowed it." Nor does it require an exchange—"Well, you look great in your outfit, too." So if you are in the habit of receiving a compliment in such a manner, perhaps you might want to get back on track with the habit of just the smile and "Thank you very much."

**ARE YOU** in the habit of giving a compliment with a question? "Is there *anything* you can't do?" sounds like a compliment, but it is not a true gift because you are expecting the recipient to give something in return. "Of course, I can't do everything—I can't cook." (The recipient might be wondering if your compliment is a sly way of telling her she makes you feel inadequate. Do you expect her to say, "No, there is nothing I can't do"? (Do you really expect *that* answer?) If you are in the habit of asking this question or a variation of it, try getting back on course with a compliment as a statement. "You seem to be able to do everything so well—I really admire that."

**IF YOU WANT** to win friends and influence people (to be *their* best), make this your next change. Cultivate the habit of giving one of the nicest gifts of all—a sincere (and honest) compliment whenever it is deserved.

## Handwritten Notes

Handwritten notes are like home-baked cookies—always appreciated. The difference, though, is that you may be able to win friends and influence people without baking, but alas, you will make fewer friends and annoy more people if you fail to write certain kinds of notes, especially thank-you notes.

Ask any person over fifty who has sent out presents in the last year to someone under thirty. "Can you believe that young people don't write thank-you notes anymore?!!" is the loud lamentation. The delicate question "Did my gift arrive?" is often a coverup for the resentment of feeling taken for granted.

While late notes are superior to unwritten—or undelivered—notes, if you want to stay on a person's good side, the way to do that is to write a thank-you note and mail it within a reasonable time. What is reasonable? One week if you want to be on someone's A-list; one month if you want to remain in the polite zone;

and better-late-than-never if you want to continue receiving gifts.

Here is a fact of life. If you are serious about improving your relationships with other people, get in the habit of writing notes—by hand—especially notes that say "Thank you," "I'm sorry," "Congratulations," and "I can really sympathize with your sorrow." Writing notes gets you in the habit of true thoughtfulness and makes you look quite special, especially as the popularity of handwriting a note wanes. Indeed, this is a habit that is easy to lose in our digital, fast-paced age but just as easy to reacquire.

So remember this maxim. *Failure* to write a thank-you note can *fail* to improve a relationship and may risk hurting one, especially with an older person. The lesson here: *When in doubt, handwrite it out.*

**HERE ARE SOME** other small changes you can make to improve your correspondence. If you use greeting cards, put some *handwriting* on them. At the very least, sign your name (even if it has been printed on the card) and *handwrite* (sorry, but yes) the address on the envelope. Add a few lines of thoughtful, handwritten prose to any greeting card, and you personalize its message.

For an important letter, such as a breakup, an apology, or a letter to inform your family that they should not have written you out of the family trust, allow yourself two to three drafts. That way you won't get hung up on the first draft, because it isn't going to get sent anyway.

Do you procrastinate about writing notes because you tend to labor over what to say? Try writing your notes on a computer, printing them out, and then handwriting what you printed onto stationery, perhaps while hanging out in a café or coffeehouse. (Store your computer thank-you note as a template for future use, but remember to change what you say about why you like the gift—and get the name right!)

None of these methods save you much time, but they make writing the note easier.

By the way, handwritten notes save you money, small change that adds up over time, as blank cards and stationery are far less expensive than greeting cards. In case we have not convinced you of the importance of a handwritten note, try this. Surprise someone by writing an overdue thank-you note or note of gratitude for something that person has done for you in the past (taken you to a sports event, written a recommendation, paid you an especially wonderful compliment) or even in the far past (been a role model, done a favor). Or:

Write to a parent, grandparent, or college friend, even if you frequently call or email them.

Leave behind a handwritten note of appreciation when you have stayed at someone's home. This leaves you with nothing to think about when you return home.

Send a note to one of your doctors after a thorough consultation.

Include a handwritten note with your tip the next time you go to the hairdresser or stay in a motel.

Brighten up a colleague's day by placing a thoughtful handwritten note on his or her desk.

For fun, write a fan letter, perhaps to someone who has delivered a great lecture or sermon or who has mentored you in some way.

Do you write notes, then neglect to mail them? Or do you have trouble getting organized? Set aside a drawer, box, vintage suitcase, or old briefcase just for your notes. (Fold-over notes, by the way, are the most versatile stationery. You can use three sides of the card for a real letter or one side for a short three-line thank you. ("Thank you for the such-and-such. I like it because . . . It was so thoughtful of you to . . .") Add a sheet of stamps. Add a glue stick, perhaps. Add a pen. Add an address book. Voila! You are over-the-top with a reliable writing kit.

While we are on the topic of writing, want to make a few small changes to improve your handwriting? The easiest change is to switch to a fountain pen, which will automatically improve the artistry of your writing. Another small change is to devote a few minutes a day to work at improving just one letter. Within a month, you will have improved almost every letter of the alphabet.

Want to improve your signature? Take a few minutes a day to experiment with it, perhaps improving only the capital letters, your initial, or adding a few good loops or a dramatic flourish at the end.

Want to write less? Practice writing larger or using wider margins.

Want to make more friends and keep the friends you have happier? Then get in the habit of writing handwritten notes. All the time. Or better late than never. Pretty straightforward.

## Voice Your Opinion

Okay. We could be coy here and keep you guessing about our politics, but we won't. Just to give you an idea of our Left-leaning tendencies, our idea of a mixed marriage is when a Democrat marries a Republican. Political parties aside, one of the most powerfully positive ways to interact within society is to voice your opinion. And yes, that means getting to the polling booth even when you have a million calls to return and hungry kids waiting for their dinner! If you have not been voting, or if you feel you could be a more informed voter, one small change that can have an enormous impact on your life and the lives of others around you is to become more involved in political debate and policy-making both on a national and local level.

Just to stop anyone dead in their tracks who says that it's not worth writing that letter to your senator or showing up at a town meeting to express your concerns, we consulted our friend's son Joshua, who is a well-respected and successful lobbyist in Washington, D.C. According to Joshua, we the people matter a great deal. Not a single political decision is made in D.C. without consideration of how it will impact the citizens of this country. After all, there are a bunch of people there who are worried about losing *your* vote! So, sign that form letter or petition, or, better yet, write your own letter, postcard, or e-mail. You might try keeping a stack of postcards, preaddressed to your senators and representatives (both national and state) and periodically, perhaps every Fourth of July, let them know what matters most to you. Elected officials realize that if you care enough to write, you probably also care enough to discuss the issue with others. And this increases the significance of your correspondence.

Take this small change a little further and learn about an issue you feel is important. Seek out other views and consider them with an open mind. Go to forums; subscribe to a journal; and read articles and books that espouse different views. If you really want to make a difference, volunteer to help someone you support get elected or re-elected. Or volunteer for an organization that lobbies for an issue you support. Loud or soft, the important thing is to make your voice heard.

## Do Something for Mother Earth

It is easy to get into the habit of taking our relationship with our Planet Earth for granted, much the way we may take personal relationships for granted—until something goes wrong or we lose them altogether. As with other areas of our lives, small changes here add up to big differences, especially when we use our personal energy to save real energy, and when our small changes set examples for others.

One of the first changes you can make is simply to become more mindful, more aware, of your relationship with the Earth. Perhaps you can get in the daily habit of studying the sky, observing the sunrise and sunset, or noting the color of the sky and the nature of the clouds during your lunch hour. Set up a bird feeder outside a window. Grow herbs in windowsill containers. Listen to the rain and wind. Anything is good that increases your *daily* awareness of the Earth and your relationship with it.

Our financially savvy and successful friend Mitch could buy any car he wants. Seriously, *any* car at all. But he doesn't. Even though he lives in a cold, snowy climate and commutes at least thirty miles every day, Mitch chooses to drive a small, hybrid car—a fuel-efficient car powered by both gas and electricity—that takes small change to a new level. We are not suggesting that the switch to a hybrid car is a small change, or that energy savings should be the only factor in selecting a car (though that isn't a bad idea). What we are saying is that being mindful of the environment requires taking energy consumption into consideration. If you don't schlepp a lot of little people or gear in your car, then consider a smaller car, and in particular a hybrid.

No matter what car you drive, you can get in the habit of making small changes that will have a cumulative effect. Such changes can save gas, save money, and do much for our small planet.

*Observe the speed limit.* You may or may not recall when the highway speed limit went down to fifty-five miles per hour *to save gasoline.* Driving at moderate speeds always saves gas.

If you are an aggressive driver, get in the habit of accelerating more slowly. If you have a heavy foot on the gas pedal, lighten up. According to the American Automobile Association, speeding, rapid acceleration, and rapid braking lower your gas mileage by thirty-three percent at highway speeds and by five to ten percent at city-driving speeds. (They also cause accidents.)

*Keep the correct air pressure in your tires.* For a few dollars you can buy an air gauge and get in the habit of frequently checking your tires—then adding air when they need it. Underinflated tires can cut a car's fuel economy by more than two percent per pound of pressure below the recommended level.

*Get in the habit of leaving yourself enough time* to get places so you don't have to rush through traffic. As we mentioned, speeding and aggressive driving can lower your gas mileage considerably.

*Get in the habit of doing more than one errand at a time.* Driving a warm car for one trip instead of starting a cold one for several short trips saves fuel. Whenever it is possible, park once and walk from errand to errand.

It helps if you get in the habit of keeping a to-do list in the kitchen. Then anyone setting out on an errand can check it and double up on what they do.

*Get in the habit of checking your air filter.* Dirty filters give the engine less air for combustion. (Think clogged noses here and how difficult it is to breathe, and you will understand exactly why.) Air and gas go together to make combustion—a simple equation:

Air + gas [combust] = power

Less air, and you need more gas to produce the same power. A dirty filter means less air, which means more gasoline.

*On the highway, use cruise control.* Maintaining a steady speed saves fuel.

*Clean the trunk and lighten the load.* The lighter the load, the less fuel the car needs to go the same distance.

*Check the brakes.* Overadjusted rear brakes waste fuel by putting more "drag" on the car, causing the engine to work harder and to use more fuel.

**ANOTHER WAY** to save energy is to get in the habit of turning off lights and appliances you aren't using. Leaving the lights on in the foyer every night for a year can consume enough electricity to burn four hundred pounds of coal, which will release almost a half ton of gases, which can contribute to both the greenhouse effect and acid rain—all from just a few light bulbs left on each day or night.

When it is cold, get in the habit of pulling down the window shades and closing the curtains to prevent heat from escaping through the window. Make small changes in your thermostat setting—a few degrees cooler in winter and warmer in summer.

*Make small changes to save water—another nonrenewable resource.* When rainfall is ample, turn off your garden sprinklers. Stop letting the water run when you brush your teeth. (You can save up to nine gallons a day this way.) Install a low-flow shower head, which can cut the consumption of water in half. Rinse dishes in a sinkful of water instead of running the water constantly down the drain.

**ANOTHER SMALL CHANGE** to benefit the Earth is to bring your own bags to the store—canvas tote bags, backpacks, or recycled store bags—whatever works for you. Keep some bags in the car and some in your house—so you have them when you actually need them. And start refusing bags for sufficiently packaged goods. (In four years, a family of four can save two fifteen-year-old trees by using their own grocery bags each week.)

The list of possible small changes may seem endless and your part in the whole scheme of things minuscule, but that you play a part at all is what matters. When it comes to the environment, you are truly part of the problem or part of the solution, however small.

Unless you are a devout environmentalist—and we applaud and respect you for that—it is difficult to observe every change all the time and difficult to always remember the change you intend to make. But if you make one change a year for Mother Earth, whether it is carrying your own shopping bags, remembering to turn off the lights, switching to a more fuel-efficient vehicle, or altering your driving patterns to use less fuel, you will be doing something positive for the largest community under the sun (and maybe in the entire universe).

## Spiritual Guidance

Would you like to know how to find comfort any time you are lonely? Courage whenever you are afraid? Guidance when you are in doubt? Inspiration when you are lost? Hope when you are down? Acquire the habit of going to a place or being with people in a way that lifts your spirit, especially when it is most in need of renewal.

For many people, this is a traditional place of worship. But spiritual renewal is also found outdoors, in the woods, on mountains, and by rivers, lakes, and seas. Others find it watching the sun rise or sitting under the night sky. Still others find it in intentional communities or retreats. Our daughter, Marni, for example, finds solace in the woods. Whenever Marni needs to clear her head and give her spirit a lift, she goes to the woods. When you retreat to a spiritual place, try to leave the nonspiritual concerns behind, as Henry David Thoreau advised. “What business do I have in the woods,” he said, “if I am thinking of something out of the woods?”

For those who cannot actually go to their sacred place, the Buddhists suggest bringing the spirit of the place to them. For practical reasons, our friend Greg cannot get to the mountains as often as he would like, so he spends time each day in the garden he created to "bring the mountain" to him, as bonsai gardening is meant to do.

In a similar vein, after two months of a horrific winter, we brought our yoga retreat in the Bahamas to our meditation room by putting up an 8-foot mural of the beach and ocean. Every time we sit in front of that scene, we feel transplanted, in our thoughts, at least, to a place that is sacred to us. We know it can not offer the comfort of an ocean breeze or the smell of fresh sea air, but nevertheless it holds the power to trigger our memories of the yoga retreat in the Bahamas where we love to vacation. And that alone lifts our spirits each day.

**THIS CHAPTER** on relationships began with the relationship you have with yourself. We conclude it with the relationships that nurture your spiritual side. These are the relationships with people whose presence in your life has the power to lift your spirits and guide you, who inspire you to be your best, do your best, and seek the best. Through either their wisdom or example, you learn when and why and how to take the high road. Through your connection to them you can grow in courage, resolve, integrity, and other qualities that will shape your character and sustain you through dark times.

Just as you need a circle of friends in everyday life, we believe in the need for a circle of love and wisdom. These people may be those we have known and loved, such as grandparents, parents, a beloved teacher, or a coach. Or they may be someone whose life we have learned to appreciate from religious practice or study, such as Jesus, Moses, Buddha, or Muhammad. They could be scholars, philosophers, or activists, such as Socrates, Henry David Thoreau, Martin Luther King Jr., or Rachel Carson. Whoever you choose is your private concern.

At the risk of sounding like New Age followers (which we admittedly are at times), Larry wants to tell you that he "hangs out" with his sages on a daily basis, thinking about how so-and-so would act or what so-and-so would say. And Susan is open to revealing that she, too, feels a close connection to her spiritual cronies. When life gets difficult, we each ponder what line of reasoning or course of action our spiritual role models might suggest. And when we are lonely or frightened, we think of them (as well as the love of our family and friends) and feel less fearful and less alone.

One small change we suggest is to post reminders of these people's teachings, or of them, to help you remember their presence in your life. Another change is to devote time during the week or, preferably, each day if your schedule permits, to deepen your relationship with them through study, contemplation, and recollection of their words and deeds.

To broaden your cadre of spiritual advisers, you can add new ones by joining a study group, reading books, or listening to tapes. Add one new teacher or role model a year, and in a decade you will have ten more people from whose wisdom you can draw.

When you cultivate spiritual relationships and deepen your spiritual practice, when you take time on a regular basis to go to the places that inspire you, whether it is actually going to them or giving yourself the quietude by evoking your memory of them, you deepen your soul and lift your spirit. You also give yourself a place to go and teachers to surround you when the chips are down. And when good fortune prevails in your life, when your soul soars, those places and people can help you stay grounded.

# 4. Small Changes for a Healthier, More Creative Mind

Our minds need as much exercise as our bodies. Given how they influence everything in our lives, from our immune system and disposition to our attitudes and perspective, they hold the key to our well-being.

With a few small changes, such as daily meditation and daydreaming, you can strengthen your mind and expand your creativity. Sustain these changes and watch your entire life improve. One section here shows how to improve your memory. You might want to make it one of your first small changes—so you can remember the small changes you want to make in all the others!

## Tame the Tube

Television is a lot like food. Too much isn't good for you. And it's best to limit the amount of junk you take in. Simple enough formula? If only . . .

As we have been saying all along, small change starts with awareness. Here it starts with an honest assessment of you and the tube. If you are a television producer, you need to watch a lot of television. If you are convalescing, you may watch a lot of television. If you feel lonely when you are home, you may use the television to provide noise or company. But a television habit that steals time away from learning about something, engaging in conversation, working on a hobby or special interest, or any of the *many* activities you never seem to have enough time for may be a wonderful place in your life to make some small changes. So if the tube has been too much in control of your time (and we don't have to administer a quiz for that—you'll *just know!*) we suggest taking small steps to tame it.

Our friend Susie and her family agreed to turn off the television for Lent one year. They discovered they had more time for talking with one another, playing games, reading, listening to music, and cultivating new hobbies. You can guess the end of this short story afterward. They decided to use the television sparingly (*very* sparingly). *Note:* They did not banish TV from their lives. What they did was tame the tube so that it would not distract from other areas of their lives.

If you think you are watching more television than you would like, or using television to fill time or as a distraction, then maybe your change for the month could be to focus on your viewing habits.

*Turn off the tube.* One suggestion is to start with one TV-free evening a week. That may be the only change you want to make. Or you might extend that evening to an entire day of TV-free living. When our children were growing up, we had TV-free evening hours—between seven and nine the TV was off. After ten it was off again, in order to make going to sleep a more attractive alternative. You might opt for a monthly weekend of TV-free living. (More than a weekend, and it is no longer a small change, although you may want to make this change—your call.)

Perhaps you are in the habit of leaving the TV on when guests arrive at your house. This is okay if they have come for a Superbowl party. Otherwise you may want to think about the effect of TV on your conversation.

*Use your VCR or digital recorder.* When you don't want to take time away from your family or when you have something more important or more exciting to do, tape the program to view at a better time. Taping gives you the advantage of fast-forwarding, which condenses the time you spend watching TV—and gives you more time for other activities.

*Scale down.* Are you among the one out of three Americans who owns at least three televisions? One small change could be to get rid of one of these, perhaps from your bedroom or dining area.

*Maintain perspective.* Remember that this book is about small change for *your* life, not someone else's life, so this may be a delicate matter if it affects other people in your household. We don't want to instigate a major confrontation. We have enough arguments over television ourselves. Larry watches some television every day; Susan watches only about twenty hours—a year!

If you are in the habit of blaming television for much of society's ills, or of being on someone's case for watching too much TV or the "wrong" shows, perhaps you should get in the habit of sealing your lips and keeping your complaints to yourself. This may not bring less TV into your life, but it could bring less conflict into it—another small change that would add up.

*Improve your TV viewing.* TV does have real importance in today's world when used well. It gives us access to information and timely, immediate pictures of world events, a "see-for-yourself" quality. The wide range of views you can find on TV give you exposure to many topics and ideas not always available in your day-to-day contacts. Whether it is anthropological studies, documentaries, ethics, culture, political debate, or alternative lifestyles, TV can bring the entire world into your living room, as well as history and a glimpse of the future. So maybe if your TV diet usually consists of sitcoms, sports, or shopping, you could use it for some armchair exploration and learning instead.

**SOME PEOPLE** choose to banish TV from their lives altogether. That, however, is not a small change, and for people who live with other people who do enjoy watching TV, both for entertainment and information, an unrealistic option. Perhaps the best advice we can offer is just this: *tame the tube.*

## Find Time to Write

We do not like to write. We like to *have written*. That said, if you have ever wanted to write a book—and didn't, ever wanted to keep a journal—and didn't; ever had ideas for stories, essays, movies, lyrics, poems, or greeting cards and failed to write them down, this advice is for you. *Find time to write.*

Why write? To reflect on your life—to help you understand, express, and explain your life. To entertain. To escape. To share. Writing helps you to clarify your thoughts and gets you in the habit of making more mindful observations, of thinking outside the box, and of deepening your contemplations.

You may have to steal time from your lunch breaks, as one aspiring (and ultimately successful) novelist did for eight years while working at a law firm. You may have to borrow time from your family, stay up later at night, or watch less television. Gift yourself anywhere from five minutes to fifteen minutes a day and you can record your musings, observations, songs, poems, or develop a manuscript or journal. If you want inspiration, look at the notebooks of Leonardo da Vinci, Virginia Wolfe, Buckminster Fuller, or Eminem—full of random thoughts and ideas. Much of what we know from our history has come from the private journals men and women have kept, often with no thought of publication.

Writing every day makes writing easier. (Not necessarily *easy* but certainly easier.) That's because writing is like any exercise: the more regularly you do it, the easier it becomes, and the better you get at it.

One timeworn saying from the Talmud, the Jewish book of commentary, says that a person's life is complete if he (or she) plants a tree, writes a book, or has a child. Planting a tree is probably the easiest to accomplish, and having a child may not be a choice or an option. But people can even write books in harsh conditions such as a prison camp or the desert. So if you *really* want to write and are living in relative comfort and luxury, you *could* write a book—a novel, memoir, or how-to book or a collection of poems, essays, or humor. It takes commitment and time, as any relationship does. Only the relationship is between you and the idea, you and the written word, you and the evolving manuscript.

Here is another tip to help you start writing. When you write a first draft, it is enough to write just a draft—it does not have to be good, and, in fact, can be horrifically bad. Don't be paralyzed by that first sentence (or word). Write the second paragraph, or the last. Remember, there are no deadlines. One Pulitzer Prize–winning author—Frank McCourt—spent *thirty years* writing his first book.

Once you have a first draft, you can always rewrite it—again . . . and again . . . and again—as most professional writers do. Anyone who has been published also has unpublished manuscripts in his or her drawers. So stop thinking about whether your writing is good or worth publishing. Do it for yourself and perhaps for your grandchildren, but if you want to *really* do it, then just do it. It is better to write a bad piece than never to have written at all.

To start writing, we suggest you take the month to get in the habit of having writing materials readily available. Remember to carry a small notepad and pen or a handful of index cards or a piece of notebook paper folded in four, or, for the modern writer, an electronic notepad—anything that will enable you to jot down a thought as soon as you get it and before it escapes.

Another habit to cultivate is to set aside a regular time each day to write—perhaps in the morning before you get out of bed, during lunchtime or a commute to work, while waiting to pick up a child, before retiring for the night—whenever you can be relatively undisturbed for at least fifteen minutes. Make this a daily practice and you will see the writing steadily add up.

We don't make any promises that your writing will be brilliant, or good, or good enough for anyone but you to read. All we know is that by getting in the habit of writing, you may begin to fulfill a personal dream, and you will exercise your mind in a way that is unique to human beings—perhaps even unique among all life forms anywhere in the universe. That is an awesome thought and something worth writing down. Oh, we just did that, didn't we?!

Maybe writing is something you want to do for the rest of your life. Maybe it is something you want to do this month and again one month each year for the rest of your life. Maybe you just want to write for a few weeks and never again. The truth is *it doesn't matter.* All that matters is that you get out of the habit of saying you are *going* to write a book someday and get in the habit of writing every day until you can say "I wrote a book" or "I started to write a book, but writing isn't my thing." Only when you discover the pain of writing can you experience the joy of not writing!

## Mental Refreshment

One of the best ways to maintain your brain is to use your brain. To stay mentally alert, many people do crossword puzzles and math problems, play bridge, and engage in other mentally challenging activities. But there is great news for those of you, like Susan, who don't enjoy these activities. Recent research suggests that people who are socially engaged also exercise their minds. Interacting with others requires use of memory, verbal skills, and, in responding to others, vision, hearing, touch, and smell.

And here is more good news. That medical myth about adult brains never getting any new cells is, well, medical myth. We acquire new neurons (brain cells) every day, and in areas of our brain where we need them most—where our highest thinking takes place. Put those new cells to work by learning something new and you will keep them. Make a commitment to be a lifelong learner of new things, whether by tasting new foods, exploring new places, finding new ideas, reading new books, listening to new music, or meeting new people. The key to stretching your mind is to put those new neurons to good use by being in the habit of learning something new *every single day.*

One small change to broaden your mental horizon is to switch your listening from AM to FM or vice versa. If you are in the habit of tuning in to a particular station, try a new one each day during the month. If you are accustomed to always ordering the same food, try new dishes or an altogether new cuisine. If you like to cook, get new cookbooks and experiment with new menus.

Take the month to explore a different part of your town or city whenever you have the chance. Learn how to play a new game or dance a new dance. Try a new hobby. Choose activities where you will meet new people—and not just new but *different.*

Read a different daily newspaper or subscribe to new journals and magazines or explore them in the library. Read books in a genre that is new for you. At the end of the month some of these new adventures may become "old friends," but that is not really the purpose. The purpose is simply to acquire the habit of learning something new *every single day* of your life. It doesn't have to be difficult or something that requires a long-term commitment. The only commitment here is to remain open to ideas, in order to keep that brain of yours well exercised.

**ANOTHER WAY TO EXPERIENCE** the world differently is to turn yourself upside down. In this way, you refresh your body and mind, and give yourself a different perspective. You can do this with one of the easiest and most important yoga positions—*Child's Pose.* For *Child's Pose,* you kneel on the floor and sit back on your knees, arms to the side, and lower your forehead to the floor. (See the illustration on page 140.) Besides stretching your hips, thighs, and ankles, this pose refreshes and calms the brain.

*Note: None of these yoga positions, and in particular the headstand and handstand, are intended for anyone with high blood pressure. Pregnant and menstruating women should*

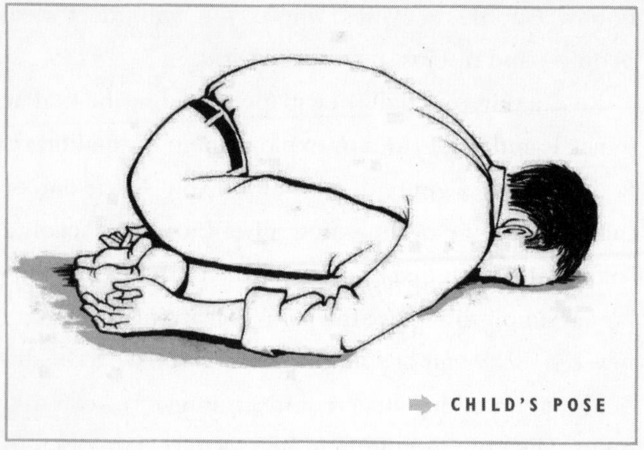

CHILD'S POSE

*also refrain from all but* Child's Pose. *We recommend that you consult your doctor and learn these postures only from a qualified yoga teacher.*

Another beneficial upside-down pose is *Downward-Facing Dog,* where you form an inverted triangle, then look at or beyond your feet.

Still another upside-down pose, regarded as the king of yoga poses, is the headstand. If you really want to rock, though, try a handstand. Thirty seconds in a handstand can increase your energy, boost your spirits, and change your attitude toward the world around you.

**OTHER WAYS OF** "seeing the world differently" are with rose-colored glasses. Seriously, get a pair of glasses in a

DOWNWARD-FACING DOG

totally unconventional shade, and you will see the world differently.

Still another daily practice is to spend a few minutes each day with your eyes closed, listening to the sounds around you (yes, for this exercise it is okay to eavesdrop). This allows you to sense the world in a different way, to increase your appreciation and awareness of both sound and sight.

Ever feel as if your brain could not process another

piece of information, confront another choice, or make another decision? That one more new idea or new memory to store will cause you to have a mental meltdown? When this occurs, as it seems to do with increasing frequency in our increasingly busy lives, the best mental refreshment you can give yourself is to sit quietly and breathe deeply, paying attention to your inhales and your exhales. Ten low, *slow,* deep breaths, and you will be mentally refreshed for the rest of the morning, afternoon, or evening. Ten low, slow, deep breaths every time you get on "overload," and you could find refreshment readily available for the rest of your life.

## Passionate Pursuits

Take a moment to reflect on your life and think about those times when you are so focused that you lose track of the clock. You are stretching your mind, expanding your creativity, or acquiring expertise in an area. When you are engaged in what we call a "passionate pursuit," your mind is calm and alert, much the way a chess master seems to be during a championship game. There may be outside rewards for such activities, from spotlights to money. Mostly, though, because engagement in passionate pursuits makes us feel so deliciously alive, at times ecstatic, we do them just for the sake of doing them.

Some passionate pursuits are relaxing, others stimulating and challenging. All inspire us to learn more, master a skill, be more creative, and occasionally to soar past our limitations. (Ask a golfer who first breaks 100, 90, or 80 how he or she is feeling about life.)

Make one of your small changes an effort to discover a passionate pursuit—an activity, hobby, or subject where time will stand still and you will be totally absorbed, if only for a few minutes each day. The best passionate pursuits lie somewhere between easy and too difficult. Too easy and you get bored; too difficult and you get frustrated. Allow yourself to pursue this new pursuit with a passion. And with no guilt, either. Being alive, working hard, and shouldering responsibilities the rest of the day entitles you to time devoted to a passionate pursuit.

If work is your passionate pursuit, count your blessings and go on to a different small change. If it isn't or if you have outgrown a job that used to excite you, find a leisure pursuit you can love, one that is challenging but enjoyable (the key here is enjoyable). If you like drawing, painting, playing the guitar, or singing, for example, commit to sketching or painting or strumming or warbling. Once you have made the commitment, carve out time from your day or week to honor the commitment to yourself. To many of you, given your busy schedules, this small change may seem like a big challenge—or indulgence. Passionate pursuits do not have to take up a lot of time (though when you love doing them, it rarely feels as if there is enough time for them). Spend just a few minutes a day if that is all you can spare, but commit to those few minutes.

Nor does a passionate pursuit have to be costly. Be creative here and consider one of our favorite mottos: *Find a Way, or Make a Way*. Have you always wanted to learn to play the piano but lacked the money for lessons or the piano? Take the month to scout around for a used keyboard and perhaps someone with whom you can barter for lessons. Susan, for example, wanted to learn to use a knitting machine but couldn't afford a new one. The day she decided to pursue this passion, she asked every single person she met if they knew anyone who had a used knitting machine. Within a few hours, someone did know someone who had quit a sweater-craft business. Within two days, Susan had the machine set up in her painting studio. She spent the better part of the month learning how to use it, along with learning how to design custom patterns. For the rest of the winter, Susan stole time (away from writing this book!) to design sweaters, search out yarn, knit, read about knitting—all this with much passion. The lesson here: set your sights, then be creative about how to reach them. (And use that magic word: *ask.*)

If you already have a passionate pursuit, your small change might be finding a way to bring it to a new level. For instance, if you are passionate about jigsaw puzzles, as our friend Andrea is, then switch to crafting them yourself for a greater challenge. Like to grow vegetables or roses? Commit to learning about vintage varieties by reading about them, finding a local group, or starting one as Fred and Linda did. They even organized group tours to farms that grow vintage varieties.

When you have more time to commit, such as a long weekend or vacation, use it to indulge yourself in your passionate pursuit. Larry often uses a long weekend or vacation to learn more about yoga, while our friend Katie devotes some of her vacation to indulging her love of knitting. Our friend Ron devotes a portion of his vacation to pursuing his passion for family genealogy, and our friends Gennie and Stephanie indulge their passion for dance by attending dance workshops and entering dance contests.

When you have invested more time or money than you like to admit, or if a hobby no longer arouses your passion, put it aside or, better yet, give your supplies to someone else who remains passionate about it. And don't feel guilty about changing hobbies (even if it's more frequently than other people change their wardrobes). Hobbies are *hobbies,* after all, not spouses. In this spirit (or with this rationalization), Susan often treats herself to a new hobby during our exceedingly long winters, knowing that the bad weather will serve as a great excuse to stay indoors and lose herself in her hobby. One year it was making miniature furniture, another year it was sorting the family photos. Still another found her (and nearly anyone else who came to visit) painting wooden candlesticks. One winter she focused on mastering the computer game FreeCell. Each of these pursuits allowed Susan to feel relaxed, happy, and most of all, wonderfully alive and creative.

**AS WE EMPHASIZE** in this book, balance and mindfulness are essential. So while we urge you to acquire passionate pursuits and harmless diversions, be aware of when a hobby becomes destructive, as when you find yourself gambling away your savings or stealing so much time from your family that you risk losing them.

In addition, while many people turn their hobbies into successful, enjoyable businesses, think twice before you succumb to the temptation. The pressure of needing to make a profit, or working under stress to complete too many projects, can cause you to lose the passion you had when your business was merely a hobby.

One last piece of advice. "Work to live; don't live to work." Even if you hate your job, or especially if you do, get in the habit of loving the rest of your life—by acquiring a passionate pursuit—and then gifting yourself permission and time to indulge in it.

## Read More

Reading more can expand your mental agility. It can also improve your ability to stave off senility—for people who use their minds tend to lose less of their minds.

We are not suggesting that you sign up for a Great Books Club (though it isn't a bad idea) or that you embark on a strict regimen of one book per week. We do suggest, however, that you read a few pages of a good book each night. Or read an op-ed piece in a national paper such as *The New York Times* or *The Wall Street Journal,* and even consider rereading it a few times until you really begin to think about the essay critically. Ask yourself these questions. Is the essay accurate? Fair? Reliable? Complete? Do you agree with what the author is saying? When you truly understand what you read, you will have more to say and more to think about. That is a small change that will yield valuable long-term results.

Start this small change by having books around that you want to read. Take one with you anytime you may have to wait for something or someone, as at the doctor's office, the car wash, the airport, or a restaurant. Put a few books in the bathroom, in the car, and next to the TV. Because here's the scoop: you don't have to finish every book you start.

**HERE'S ANOTHER** small change. Simply read a few more pages, say one to three, than you are currently reading. If you read a lot but it is all for entertainment, then upgrade your reading by reading a few books for knowledge or understanding. Get a collection of essays, for example, and read one or two essays a week. Buy the *History of Civilization* and read one to three pages a night—when the year is over, you will have read quite a bit of it, and if you hadn't started the habit, you would have read none of it. Want to go short? Make your small change just one poem a day or night for one month or perhaps a few lines a day. Or read one Shakespeare play, even one you have read before. (You may see things differently this time around.)

*Read one page a day for three hundred days of the year and you will have either read one average book, three short books, or half of one tome.*

*Read two pages a day for 350 days of the year and you will read seven hundred pages more: at least five short books, two to three average books, one long book, or half of the* History of Civilization *(or its equivalent).*

Can't think of what to read? Like to gamble? Read a book on statistics. Nosy about people? Read a biography or memoir. Like to collect antiques? Why not learn about a specific period, such as colonial America? Is cooking your thing? Read a book about nutrition or food in history.

Here are some other ideas: read the "staff picks" at the bookstore; ask a librarian for suggestions; get a reading list from a college course on literature or history. Read those diverse lists of National Book Award or Pulitzer Prize finalists, which will include fiction and nonfiction, poetry, memoir, biography, and perhaps collections of short stories or essays. Read serious magazines and journals that introduce important, timely topics, new writers, and diverse views such as *The Atlantic Monthly, Harper's, The Nation, The New Republic,* and *Partisan Review.*

Pick a favorite author and then read everything, starting with the first book, in that author's career.

Join a book discussion group or start one of your

own. Can't find one? Call your local bookstore or library—they are bound to know of several.

The point here is to get in the habit of reading just a little more each day, to read better books, to learn more, to think more. If it helps stave off senility, too, what's so bad about that?

## Improve Your Vocabulary

If improving your vocabulary sounds too much like trying to ratchet up your SAT scores or transform yourself into a Scrabble pro, think again. Just as savory ingredients, exquisite garnishes, and wonderful herbs enhance the food we eat, a fine vocabulary can add clarity, wit, and even drama to what we say and write. Fresh expressions, too, spice up a conversation.

A better vocabulary will help you speak more clearly and concisely. Skill in communicating lessens the chance of misunderstandings and improves your chance of smoothing out those that do occur.

If you are accustomed to swearing, you are probably using the same swear words over and over again. Why not freshen up your fighting skills with creative insults?

*One new word a week adds fifty-two words to your vocabu-*

*lary in a year. One new verb a month (verbs being the secret to vibrant writing), and in a decade you will have enriched your speech and writing in 120 ways.*

A richer vocabulary animates, adds vitality, enlivens, and adds precision and color, or energy, spirit, and art, to communicating—and new words are free. In the course of conversation, you can pick up new words from your friends and the people you meet. Ask them for interesting, unusual words. A word you get in this way usually leaves a more lasting impression than a word you choose from the dictionary—because your connection to the person you know strengthens your use of it.

For example, when Susan asked her friend Sally for a word to add to her vocabulary, she gave her "sartorial." Susan recalls: "I was sitting in Sally's kitchen, in her old house that was once the home of the brother of abolitionist John Brown, who organized a raid on the government arsenal at Harper's Ferry, Virginia, and was tried and hanged for treason, inciting a slave revolt. There, in that home rich in memories and history, in Sally's newly renovated kitchen, I received the word *sartorial.* How could I, someone who loves clothes, ever forget that gift?" It is a gift Susan loves to pass on. "*Sartorial* expression," she'll say, and casually add, "the way you express yourself with your clothing."

The average person knows ten thousand words, but

when talking or writing uses fewer than half of them and, in many cases, only two thousand. If you want to make use of this otherwise useless statistic, consider this small change. Start using some of the words you know but never use. Whenever you hear a word in conversation, and especially when you read one you know but do not ordinarily use, write it on a scrap of paper. As soon as you find time, write that word in three different sentences, and we assure you, it will find its way into your speaking vocabulary.

Of course, the old-fashioned but sure way to improve your vocabulary is to read material that stretches it. And the easiest material to work from is the newspaper—always available and even disposable. Cut out an article with one to three words you either don't know or don't ordinarily use. Look them up in the dictionary, then write your three sentences, and voila! they will be yours.

Why stop at English words? Try to learn a few new words in another language. Spend each week on a different language and then learn just one word a day—hello, good-bye, pardon me, please, and thank you. In one month you can be polite in four different languages!

**REMEMBER THAT PILOT** who wandered off course and headed for the wrong destination? Vogue words or trendy locutions from TV, movies, and other popular culture creep into our lexicon and take us off course. They may sound fresh at first but quickly fade to trite, tired, overused, and quickly dated words. Like. Whatever. Duh. Hello?! Not. Get *ooooouuuuut.* You know, get the picture?

Bad grammar habits can also take us off the course of polished speaking. One example is the use—or rather, misuse—of pronouns. Not so long ago, it seemed that most people knew how to use a pronoun correctly. Then, like a contagious virus, pronoun misuse crept into popular speech.

"Me and him [*note:* correct use is *He* and *I*] are going to the concert."

"Come shop with Sally and I" (with Sally and *me*).

"It was him." "It was her." (It was *he.* It was *she.*)

Every year, Susan is in the habit of following one rule from what is probably the nation's smallest but easiest grammar book, Strunk and White's *Elements of Style.* Five years ago we learned to use "that" and "which" correctly.

But don't get too stuffy! The point is to become more free and creative in your speech and in your writing. Actually, this year we intend to take a break from grammar and concentrate on some other small changes because we suspect we're beginning to sound like English teachers or overly concerned parents. *Give me a break,* you may be saying by now. *Whatever.*

Hey, give yourself a break and go after one of those freebies in life—new words or better grammar. But remember—only one change at a time.

## Imagine That

From the dream of soaring into space, preventing polio and other diseases, inventing wireless communications and personal computers to constructing the world's tallest buildings, we are daydreamers whose dreams defy all odds. As human beings, when we blend tenacity and hard work with imagination, even our wildest dreams can come true.

By holding fast to the dream of a better life for their children and themselves, millions of immigrants have found the will to keep going despite hard lives. Nearly every successful actor, rock star, athlete, artist, and entrepreneur started out with a dream. From the chance of winning a lottery to the notion of becoming a celebrity, dreams fill our lives with optimism, hope, and happiness.

Through daydreams we find the incentive to work toward difficult goals. Through daydreams we muster the courage to face hardships, as well as the vision to overcome obstacles. Any prisoner of war or shipwreck survivor will attest to the power of daydreams.

Okay, enough of the pep talk. Here is the small change. Commit some time, perhaps each day or at the beginning or end of each week, to use your imagination for daydreaming. If you have time, keep a record of your daydreams for future reference. If you already have a dream, use the month to visualize the dream more clearly, perhaps to note whatever it might take to make that dream a reality.

**IMAGINATION** is an excellent tool for improving yourself. Our son Ari, for example, would daydream about skiing. He'd practice "helicopter" turns off the bed (ours, of course). He'd spend time imagining himself in a ski race, visualizing how to take every gate or ski down an icy patch. When winter came, his skiing improved, not only from actual practice but from the off-season imaginary "practice" through visualization and daydreaming. Like Ari, you can get into the habit of visualizing the skill and form you need for skiing or another athletic activity, such as archery, that requires coordination and a mind-body connection. You can also use visualization to improve painting, design, flower arranging, or architecture.

All our lives—especially in school and at work—we are taught to stay focused and on task, especially when faced with a big project or tight deadline. Our small-change advice: when the going gets tough, get going, but also take "timeouts"—to let your mind relax and rejuvenate. Although this advice may seem counterproductive, sometimes it is *exactly* what is needed when there is a tight deadline, important decision to make, or job to do. When you allow, and especially when you encourage, your mind to relax and meander, its musings often hold the "answers" to your questions, sometimes as if by magic. Or the time you take "not-thinking" about something is precisely when an epiphany occurs. In fact, the history of invention and discovery, from Thomas Edison and Albert Einstein to the invention of Post-it notes, is full of such mental breakthroughs.

Allowing your mind to wander is an essential part of the creative cycle. You may feel as if you have abandoned your "real" work when you take time off from it, but often this is when new ideas or a fresh perspective bubble up in your mind or appear in a mental flash.

When Susan is in one of those "incubation" cycles of creativity, she does mindless tasks, such as organizing a junk drawer, cooking, or mending clothes, that allow her to clear her mind or let it wander. For someone else it could be weeding, working on the car, or painting a room. During these activities her most creative ideas appear, often one right after another.

**GET OVER THE IDEA** that unless you have the talent, time, or means to make a dream come true, you should abandon it. True, the bigger the dream, the greater the need for diligence, hard work, and lucky breaks. Daydreams do *not* require reality checks, however. In fact, what may destroy dreams *are* reality checks! Therefore, if you are in the habit of giving your own or someone else's daydreams a reality check, think again. You may be suffering from Black Cloud Disease (otherwise known as raining on a parade), a habit you can break—through awareness. For as the poet Robert Browning so eloquently explained, "Ah, but a man's reach should exceed his grasp, or what's a heaven for?" Without daydreams, most people would neither contemplate nor achieve one of life's biggest thrills: the experience of fulfilling a wild dream. Even watching someone else have the experience provides a vicarious thrill.

Speaking of vicarious thrills, do you often envy the fulfillment of other people's dreams or feel disappointment or despair when you compare your life to theirs? Unless they truly inspire you, stop reading or watching stories about other people's success. Instead, use the time for working toward the fulfillment of your own dreams.

Take long walks and reimagine your life. Restore the lost childhood art of lying in the grass, looking up into the clouds, and daydreaming about life. Relax in a hot bath and daydream.

Remember: it is through imagination that we can start our futures, through imagination that we can establish our potential, through imagination that we can set our goals, and through imagination that we begin to make the impossible possible.

**WHAT IF DAYDREAMING** isn't your "thing"? Your small change this month could be more mindful observation. Make observation a daily habit, and it will add up to hours of clarity. You'd be surprised what you see when you take the time to really look. If you are accustomed to focusing on what you see, switch gears and start to focus on what you hear and smell.

Study the flowers in a garden as though preparing to paint them in detail like Georgia O'Keeffe. Take up birdwatching and listen to the conversation of birds. Easier still, engage in serious people-watching. Study faces and look hard at the particular way people gesture, their silent modes of communication, their gait.

Our friend Ann, for example, can identify and imitate just about any walk (she has our daughter Marni's bounce down perfectly).

Will such observation get you "ahead in life"? Perhaps—if you are an artist, actor, director, psychologist, writer, or detective. For everyone else, being more observant can add a dimension to what we see, make life far more interesting, and give our minds an awareness we would otherwise not possess.

## Explore Your Dreams

You will spend approximately a third of your life—as many as 250,000 hours—sleeping! And much of that time is spent dreaming, making sleep—and your dreams—a great place to make a small change in your life.

Not all, and perhaps not even most, dreams can give you insight into problems and dilemmas. But some do, and besides, if you are going to spend so much of your mental life sleeping and dreaming, why not pay attention to your dreams?

Many people let a constant river of worries course through their minds at night, which can prevent sleep or cause nightmares. Even when your day went well, and especially when it didn't, the following habits can relax your brain before it gets its big sleeptime workout.

Say a prayer.
Think of at least one nice thing that someone said or that happened to you during the day.
Recall a favorite place and imagine being there.
Take several low, slow, deep breaths (always a good idea).

If you still find yourself tossing and turning, switch on a tiny light and read or listen to soft music on the radio. (We have other ideas, but this is a chapter on dreaming, and besides, some of our ideas would give this an R rating.)

**FROM TIME** immemorial people have attempted to interpret dreams. One of the most famous of all dreamers, the biblical Joseph, used his dreams to save others from famine and ultimately himself from a wretched life in bondage. Others "see" winning lottery numbers in their dreams. Still others discover solutions to problems they have tackled during the day. Naturally, we can't promise such successful outcomes, but we can promise you that getting in the habit of remembering your dreams will put you in better touch with your mind, your personality, and your life.

The best way to do this is to get in the habit of keeping a notebook next to the bed. Whenever you awaken from a dream, jot down a few elements of the dream. Our friend Bernice, an artist, sketches her dreams and uses them as the basis for paintings, as artists and writers have often done.

In the morning, think about what your dreams may stand for or may be telling you. With practice and consistency, you will learn to go beyond the literal meaning of your dreams and their "plots" and characters and settings. In fact, you may find that remembering, recording, and interpreting your dreams improves your dream landscape, making your dreams more lucid and more vivid.

To help you interpret your dreams, you could consult dream interpretation books (or spend a few years in analysis). But these books list "suggested" interpretations. While there are common symbols that seem to surface in dreams across many cultures and times, each person's dreamscape is unique—blending individual personalities, characteristics, emotions, life experiences, and the like. In the long run, therefore, the person who holds the ultimate key to your mind and to its dreamscape is yourself.

Plagued with nightmares? Try this small change: rewrite them. If people can distort their memories, certainly you can distort a bad dream. So when you dream that someone is chasing you, upon awakening (or, if you can, while you are actually dreaming) change that person's identity to that of someone you trust. Imagine that person is chasing you to tell you something good. If you dream of dangling over a bridge or falling down a steep embankment, make the scene an amusement park. When you dream of having loose teeth or being naked (common nightmares), as soon as you awaken, rewrite the scene and give yourself teeth that are strong and clothing that is sensational. Rewriting your dreams in this way gives your brain the message that during sleep nothing is permanent. With practice, you may eventually train your mind to revise nightmares as they are occurring.

**THE BEST PART** about recording your dreams is the rich harvest of ideas they provide for you to think about in your waking hours—or better yet, to write about, paint about, and make movies about. And maybe, as was true for Andrew Lloyd Weber when he wrote *Joseph and the Amazing Technicolor Dream Coat,* something to make music about.

# Go for It

**WE HAVE THREE (TRUE) STORIES WE WANT TO TELL YOU.**

**STORY 1** concerns Robert Fritz, a music student who was studying the clarinet at the Boston Conservatory of Music. His very first assignment was difficult; even after a week of practice, Robert had not mastered the piece. No matter; his teacher assigned him a *more* difficult piece, and in the following weeks even harder pieces, all of which seemed beyond his skill.

At the sixth lesson, Robert's teacher asked him to play the first assignment. To his surprise, he played it well now, and he could play the second week's piece well, too.

Stretching your mind to learn new skills is challenging. With persistence, however, you can go beyond what you ever thought was possible for you to achieve. Success need not be achieved at first, nor should you let failure hold you back. Keep trying. It is not necessary to master one thing before moving on to another. Don't ever get stuck on what seems to be a difficult small change. Move on to another. By the time you have made several small changes, you may find the one that was once so hard is now easy.

Try this for a small change. Each day challenge yourself to practice something that is difficult for you. Allow yourself to enjoy the process and not dwell on the outcome. In time, like Robert, you may look back at what you once thought was difficult and amaze yourself by how easy it has become.

Mastering what we think we cannot do is a wonderful way to develop self-esteem. Through such experiences our minds grow and our spirits soar.

**STORY 2** is about Sri Chinmoy, an Indian yoga master. Sri Chinmoy decided to make simple line drawings of birds—and committed to doing one hundred thousand of them! By the time he completed that many bird drawings, he had become an artist.

His story has inspired the Terkel "One Thousand Horses" Theory of Learning: if you know nothing about painting and nothing about horses and paint one thousand horses, or ten thousand, or, as Sri Chinmoy did, one hundred thousand, you will understand both painting and horses.

**STORY 3** is a report on a survey of classical musicians. While love of music and talent probably inspired them to be musicians, the survey showed that those who had practiced approximately ten thousand hours during their youth were accomplished enough to join community symphony orchestras, while those who had practiced an average of twenty thousand hours had achieved a higher professional level and were members of high-level professional orchestras. Those who had practiced in excess of thirty thousand hours achieved the highest status in the music world.

The lesson here is obvious. Regardless of talent or passion, the more you work at something, the better you get at it. Or, as the old adage goes, practice makes perfect. And this too: it takes daily practice over years to achieve excellence. Even athletes like Tiger Woods, with all their natural talent, need to practice, practice, practice.

**DOES THIS** little exchange sound familiar?

**PERSON 1:** I would *love* to be a(n) (*fill in the blank, but here are some suggestions:* artist, chef, musician, surfer, mountain climber), but I have no talent. (*Or:* I'm not good enough.)

**PERSON 2:** Have you ever tried?

**PERSON 1:** No, but . . .

We say: forget the "but" and *go for it.* Who says you have to have talent to do something you want to do?

Clearly, what many people lack in talent they make up in the sheer joy of going for what they always wanted to do.

One small habit in particular stands in the way of many people. This is the habit of criticism. If you want to be happy and go for it, then banish the critics from your life, including your own critical self, as well as anyone else who steals your confidence. How? Try this little habit that our friend Bernice adapted from Native American customs and taught Susan. *Bury the critic.* Whenever Susan feels insecure about writing or painting, she visualizes putting Barbara-the-editor-who-once-wrote-her-a-scathing-rejection into an imaginary box, then visualizes burying the box outside the door of her writing room. When she needs to banish her seventh-grade art teacher who told her mother she had no artistic talent, Susan visualizes posting that remark *outside* the door to her painting studio. And there the critics remain while Susan happily writes and paints away the hours.

Give yourself permission to do bad, really bad, stuff. Even if you have talent (or especially if you do), giving up the idea that everything you do has to be good or everything you start has to be finished gives you the freedom to explore, be more creative, and go off in entirely new directions. *Failure to give yourself this freedom* is a pathway to blocks or to the abandonment of your creative work altogether.

As we suggested in our chapter on writing, it is better to practice something every day than wait for inspiration to strike. Why not make this month the month for trying something you have always wanted to do? And remember—give yourself permission to be bad, as Robert did from lesson to lesson; patience to stick with it, as Sri Chinmoy did through one hundred thousand drawings; and the passion to continue doing what you love, no matter what anyone thinks or says about your work, as Susan does. Practice long enough, and you will achieve *something*. You may never achieve the status of Van Gogh or Grandma Moses, but you will join the ranks of the can-doers instead of the yes, but-ers. In short, be reasonable about your expectations, lengthen your learning curve, banish your critics—and "go for it!"

## Keep an Open Mind

Since we are on a story kick, here's another true story that inspires us. As you read it, consider what you would do in the same circumstance.

This story happened in Chester, Pennsylvania, during a time of economic and social unrest in the 1960s. In an older, deteriorating section of Chester stood a building owned by a Quaker meeting in which they ran a community center. The Quakers are a religious denomination known for ways of peace. (The Quaker William Penn named the city he founded—Philadelphia—the city of "brotherly love.")

One day a group of African-American activists marched into the building, refusing to leave and demanding that the Quakers relinquish control of the center to them. The members of the Quaker meeting were surprised and upset by the tactic, as well as the demands. Despite their anger, however, they decided to send a small delegation to confer with the organizers of the occupation. And here is the twist. The Quakers went, not to state their claim or to evict anyone, either forcefully or persuasively. They went simply with the intention of gathering information and hearing the arguments of the people who were demanding control of the building and the community center in it.

Soon afterward the Quakers invited a delegation of the occupiers to attend their meeting. Over many months—and months—and months—the situation was discussed among the members of the Quaker meeting. When the discussion became heated, all talk would cease and the group would sit in silence, searching their minds and hearts for the right thing to do.

Ultimately, the Quakers decided to relinquish control of the community center and even volunteered to help run it.

The purpose of this story here is to suggest a small change. If you tend to jump to conclusions before gathering as much information as possible, or if you often listen to different ideas with a closed mind, then you might consider the effect on your life of striving to make objective decisions, showing compassion and understanding for those who hold different viewpoints, and keeping your mind open so that you can open your heart.

You don't have to be a Buddhist to understand that when the cup is full, there is no room left for anything new. When your mind is "full," when you think you know everything, there is no room left for new ideas, fresh perspectives, or seeking out the truth. Worse, when you stubbornly hold on to your ideas without seeing the entire picture, you risk missing an opportunity to reconcile a difficult situation or bring a peaceful solution to a contentious issue.

One small change to make, therefore, is to shift from being set in your ways to being open to new ideas, from being defensive to being amenable, from being opinionated to being inquisitive, from being doctrinaire to being able to compromise.

One way to maintain an open mind is to constantly expose your mind to alternative viewpoints. Include both conservative and liberal writers in your reading; befriend people whose views are different from your own, even radically different. Such differences can be the most refreshing part of an evening discourse.

Cultivate the habit of asking questions, being tolerant, and staying open-minded, and you will have a lifetime of expanding thoughts, new ideas, and a fresh look on life. You may end up with a cup half full, but consider this—you will constantly be upgrading to a larger and larger cup to hold your expanding viewpoints and growing wisdom.

## Work on Your Memory

In bygone days, memorizing poems, passages, prayers, and speeches was a valued activity, as was reciting them. Today, though, as politicians and actors rely on Teleprompters instead of memory, and as educators balk at rote memory, recitation claims few supporters. We happen to be among those few, however, who regard memorization and recitation as a useful habit that can exercise your brain, and that over time will add up to some delightful dividends.

Besides giving your brain a mental workout, memorization will help you with the opportunity to inspire or entertain others. And when you memorize a well-written, lyrical passage or poem, you improve the vocabulary and cadence of your own speech.

Devote the first week for this small change simply to finding what you would like to memorize. Browse through collections of poetry, short stories, speeches, or monologues. Pick up some sheet music or use the lyrics on a CD cover. Mine a book of jokes or quotations for material. Search through a prayer book, Bible, novel, play, or movie script.

After you have made your selection, read (or sing) the words until you feel comfortable with them, completely understand them, and can put some feeling into reciting them. Now you are ready to begin memorizing.

We offer you different ways to memorize, all of which we learned from our friend Neil, a former drama teacher who owns and runs our local theater with his wife, Mary Jo. One system is for auditory learners—those who need to *hear* what they are going to memorize. The other system is for visual learners—those who need to actually *see* the words or lyrics.

If you are unsure of which system to use, ask yourself this: Do you remember someone's name when you hear it, or do you have to see it written on a nametag, business card, or placecard or actually visualize its spelling in your mind?

**FOR AUDITORY LEARNERS.** Read the piece aloud several times. When you are satisfied with your delivery, read it into a recording device. Now, here's the secret that Neil taught us: record only one or two lines at a time. Then pause long enough so that you will have time to repeat those lines when you listen to the recording later. Record the same lines aloud once more. Now go to the next line or two and repeat this process of lines-pause-lines.

When you are ready to actually memorize, play the first lines you had recorded. During the pause, repeat them aloud. Now listen to the lines on the recording once more, noting which words or phrases you forgot or got wrong.

Only move to the next lines after you have perfectly memorized the previous ones. This means that unless you have a photographic memory, you will have to rewind the tape or CD to go over the first lines again and again until you have memorized them exactly, *word for word,* as the writer wrote them. The reason to avoid paraphrasing, claims Neil, is that it causes you to break your concentration when you need to concentrate the most.

Once you have memorized a section, go on to the next section. Occasionally you can test your memory by writing down what you recite and checking it with the original copy.

**FOR VISUAL LEARNERS.** You will still need to recite the passage aloud and to hear your own voice before you begin to memorize it. (This is an important step because, according to Neil, even visual learners need to "hear" the words, since they will eventually be speaking them.)

Read a line or two, then cover it with an index card or paper. Now recite what you just read. Afterward, remove the paper and reread (aloud) the line you just recited. Repeat these steps until you have memorized, again, word for word, the entire passage. If you are memorizing a song, you will be singing it.

Now you are ready to go on to the next line. If you are good at memorizing, you may want to do a paragraph at a time, but Neil suggested refraining from doing more than that at one time.

Spend a few minutes a day on this, ideally before going to sleep, since your brain stores more memory during sleep than at any other time. In a short time you will have a growing repertory of material. The real fun begins with reciting it—in the car or shower, on a walk or run, and eventually to others.

**IF WORDS DON'T** move you, spend time memorizing music. Or acquiring a better ear. According to our son's friend Paul, who is a jazz musician and trombonist, you can acquire relative (the next best thing to perfect) pitch by playing one note, then pausing to hear exactly what it sounds like. Play it again and "correct" your memory of it. Do this until you can remember exactly what it should sound like. Practice a note or two each week, and by the end of the year you will be able to discriminate the notes, as well as hear a note and know what that note is. This in turn will help you to appreciate good music and improve your own music-making.

**WORDS AND SOUNDS** don't inspire you to memorize? Here's an exercise to improve both your ability to remember and your visual acuity. This, in fact, is an exercise the artist and inventor Leonardo da Vinci used to practice.

Study a floral arrangement, the architecture of a building, a painting, or whatever you would like to remember. Choose something that is somewhat visually complex. Then close your eyes, and try to reconstruct what you have just seen. Next, open your eyes and compare your visual memory to the actual object, building, or artwork—whatever you studied—looking closely, and carefully correcting your memory. Close your eyes again and try to visually reconstruct what you saw. Repeat this exercise until your visualization matches what you see—exactly.

**WITH ALL THESE** exercises you sharpen your mind, as well as your ears and eyes. You also gain a growing repertoire of passages, poems, jokes, quotations, songs, music, and marvelous works of art to recall and perhaps recite and share with others—an increasingly rare and special gift.

## The Natural High

Few small changes in your daily routine can improve your mind and even the rest of your body as much as meditation. It lowers blood pressure, calms the mind, adds clarity, unlocks creativity, and promotes harmony and perspective. As little as ten to twenty minutes spent in daily meditation can bring peace and energy to the rest of your day. It helps compensate for a lack of sleep and is a great substitute for a nap. Yes, we are confident of these claims, and if you don't believe us, then trust the large body of medical research that supports them.

Just as there are numerous ways to exercise, stretch, and relax your body, there are many ways to meditate. We invite you to try the following meditation technique, which Larry has been practicing and teaching for over thirty years.

**STEP 1.** *Find a place.* Find a quiet, peaceful place where you are unlikely to be distracted. You may wish to add soothing music, incense, candles, or an altar to make it feel special, but nothing is required, and with practice, you *can* learn to meditate anywhere, even in a place as noisy as Grand Central Station!

**STEP 2.** *Sit in a comfortable position, with your spine as straight as possible.* If you sit on the floor, use a firm pillow that raises your seat close to the level of your knees (in a crossed-leg position; see the illustration). Or, if it is more comfortable for you, tuck your legs under you and sit on the heels of your feet.

If you choose to sit in a chair, give your lumbar region support by either using a pillow to support your lower back or by sitting forward on the front edge of

SITTING POSE FOR MEDITATION

the chair. If you want to meditate sitting up in bed, put a pillow behind your lower back, again to support the lumbar curve and strengthen the spine.

Place your hands, palms up, on your knees or on your lap, one hand over the other, with thumbs gently touching (see the illustration above).

**STEP 3.** *Relax.* Spend a minute or so relaxing your body. One technique is to tense all the muscles in your body and then, during an exhalation, release the tension, paying attention to relaxing the areas where we tend to hold the most tension—the stomach, shoulders, and face.

At the end of this short relaxation, Larry likes to vigorously rub his palms together to generate warmth and energy. He also stimulates the top of his head by lightly scratching it with his fingernails to create a tingling sensation that brings focus and attention there.

**STEP 4.** *Select a mantra.* Larry uses a two-syllable *mantra*—a word, phrase, or sound to help focus the mind. A mantra may have a spiritual, philosophical, or emotional meaning or may be simply a sound or vibration.

To find a mantra, Larry suggests that you "listen" to your breath to find a two-syllable sound created by your inhale and exhale. This sound will become your mantra. Try several mantras until you find one that "sounds like" your breathing. If you can't find a mantra that does, you may want to try a different technique.

Here is a short list of two-syllable mantras you could try.

A-men

God's love

heal-ing

Je-sus (pronounced in Spanish "heh"-sus)

bless-ing

Ma-ry

I-am

di-vine

lov-ing

Sha-lom (Hebrew for *peace*)

Al-lah (Arabic for *God*)

sat-nam (Arabic for *Truth is God's name*)

so-hum (Sanskrit for *That which is*)

A two-syllable mantra is easiest to use, but you may prefer a longer mantra, such as one found in a religious prayer. A classic Tibetan Buddhist mantra, for example, is *Om Mani Padme Hum* (oh-mmmmm mah-knee pod-mu [as in "mud"] hummmmm), which means "the jewel is in the lotus." Such mantras are not as easy to harmonize with your breathing but, with practice, can become quite natural.

**STEP 5.** *Meditate on your mantra.* Listen to your breathing and "hear" the mantra you have selected. If you have chosen "Amen" as your mantra, hear the breath whisper "ahhh" on the inhale and "men" on the exhale. As the breath is "whispering" this gentle mantra, repeat the mantra in your mind. Now, take this duet of breath mantra and mind mantra and imagine it resonating in your heart, in your throat, in your forehead, or at the top of your head. Do this for approximately five to ten minutes.

While you are hearing and thinking and feeling your mantra, you may feel your blood pressure drop, your breathing grow shallow, and your body become still. Good, but not required. Thoughts may come into your mind. Tension or discomfort may return or develop as you sit. This is okay. For meditation is also a witnessing of these physical sensations and thoughts. So be gentle with the process. Witness such distractions with mild bemusement, "exhale" them away, and return to hearing your mantra.

If you have an itch, scratch it; then return to your mantra. If you feel the need to check the time, open your eyes, check the time, and return to your mantra. Avoid turning these distractions into a big deal. Simply return to your enjoyment of the mantra.

**STEP 6.** *Leaving meditation.* Come out of meditation and return to the world, so to speak, as gently as you can. First, deepen your breathing to bring yourself enough energy to move. You may want to lower your chin into a position of gratitude, and perhaps invoke a personal prayer at this time.

Then, begin gently stretching your body. When you are ready, slowly open your eyes. You may feel awe, appreciation, amazement, and wonder at this stage.

During meditation the "rational mind" slows down while the "creative mind" is free to flourish. Often during meditation solutions to problems emerge or become clearer; novel ideas float up and appear. Larry keeps a pad of paper nearby for recording the thoughts and ideas that come to him during or immediately after meditation.

**WE ENTER MEDITATION SLOWLY.** Leaving meditation slowly helps us to maintain its inner peace, and to experience its higher consciousness for as long as possible.

Every meditation experience is different. Harmony ebbs and flows. The purpose of meditation is not to switch off our minds but to bring the orchestration of body, mind, heart, and spirit into harmony. Therefore, try to avoid seeing meditation in the same way you may look at exercise. It is not a challenge to do better or best—compared to yourself or anyone else. Trust that with practice your meditation experience will deepen, and the benefits of meditation will accumulate. Let meditation teach you how to follow, to listen, and to find harmony and peace within yourself. Mantra meditation becomes your tune—the tune of your soul. Learn to *hummmmmmmm* and enjoy its music.

# 5. Small Change at Work

Whether you work for yourself or someone else, part-time or full-time, outside the home or inside, for a paycheck or no pay, small change can make a big difference in your life. In this chapter you will find suggestions for improving your life at work.

We included enough ideas for change to inspire you to make many small changes. Remember, though, *only one at a time*—because slow and steady won the race for the tortoise. And slow and steady can improve your life when you make small change a constant, especially when your work is a large part of your life.

## What Are You Doing and Why Are You Doing It?

We all want work we can enjoy, work that makes a difference to people, and work that pays us gobs and gobs of money. But let's get real. How many people have jobs or careers that give them three out of three on this wish list?

The research scientist working on a cure for a rare disease may earn one-twentieth of the earnings of his or her medical school classmate who is performing elective plastic surgery, but that does not make the researcher's job less valuable to society. As our friend Joshua Halberstam, the author of a book entitled *Work,* explains, "The value of our work is judged not by its success in the marketplace but by the integrity with which we bring it there." So whether it is a profession for which you trained for years, or a job as a computer technician, or staying at home to take care of a child or elderly parent, work feels more meaningful when you appreciate the value of what you are doing.

When you ask yourself what are you doing and why are you doing it, the answers may change the way you value your work. They may help you find more meaning in the job you have, a small change that makes a big difference in the way you feel about your work. Here are some suggestions.

*Begin with a job description.* See how your work fits in the "big picture." You can find the meaning of your work when you see its place in a larger context. Remember this folktale?

For want of a nail, the shoe was lost;
For want of a shoe, the horse was lost;
For want of a horse, the rider was lost;
For want of a rider, the battle was lost;
For want of a battle, the kingdom was lost!

A young woman enters a salon. She is tall, overweight, and slightly frumpy. The hair color that she has been doing herself is wrong for her skin tone. Her hairstyle doesn't flatter her face or her figure.

First you change the color and then you show her different styles before selecting one that you both agree is attractive. As you blow-dry her hair and curl the ends under, sweeping your fingers through to fluff it out, you see the smile appear on her face; you see her shoulders straighten. You see her admire herself in the mirror. You see her strut out the door, confident and feeling great.

How do you see yourself, though? As just a hairdresser? Or do you see the bigger picture and understand that you are also a stylist, therapist, cheerleader, and coach when you help transform her into a happier woman? Imagine the effect of her transformation—when she happily chats with the person she encounters on her next errand, when she prepares dinner for her family at night, and when she sees her colleagues at work the next day.

From the mechanic who tightens the brakes on a car that a family's breadwinner—a sales representative—drives safely across the state on a business trip to the person who flips burgers and helps to feed nine hundred busy people lunch each day, seeing work in a larger context adds meaning.

Maybe your job doesn't benefit a lot of others. Maybe you are writing a script that will never get sold, never go into production, never be seen by anyone but yourself. If you are supporting yourself, and if you find meaning in what you do, that is meaning enough.

Of course, there is always your immediate family who benefit from your paycheck. That little baby who smiles when you come in the door . . . now that's meaning.

One small change, therefore, is to see your work in the big picture of life. Make a list, if you will, of all that you do for work and all the people whose lives you affect, both directly and indirectly. See the effect of your work on the present and in the future. Keep this list where you can read it if you need a reminder of why you are doing what you do.

Write yourself a mission statement. When you can be clear about what you do and why you do it, we think you will be better able to stay on course or get back on course if you have gone astray.

Try to understand why you do the work you do. Matthew doesn't particularly love selling decorative hardware. But the job enables Matthew and his family to have a comfortable lifestyle, and it gives him the added emotional benefit of working with his father, who is trustworthy, dependable, and knowledgeable. On one level, like many others, Matthew is working for a paycheck. It may not be his dream job, but it offers certain advantages that he is not willing to give up.

On the other hand, we believe it is impossible—and wrong—to rationalize work that violates basic codes of decency, such as work that may have negative consequences for people, the environment, or the future.

Once you are clear about exactly why you are doing what you are doing, write a mission statement of purpose for yourself and your current work. If you have trouble doing this, you may want to start exploring other kinds of work to do. Or, if you complain about your work a lot, your mission statement may help you see it in a more realistic perspective.

Periodically reread your job description and mission statement or commit them to memory. Bear in mind, though, that this exercise is not about job counseling or finding the perfect line of work. It is about improving your perspective on the work you already do—to understand it more clearly and appreciate it more fully.

When you are in the habit of seeing what you do in a larger context and knowing exactly why you are doing it, you will appreciate your work—or start looking for work that you can appreciate. That is all. (Small change, remember?)

## Who Is *Your* Employer?

Many of you are self-employed. The rest of you are also self-employed. Questionable logic? Not when you consider a certain small change you can make in the way you perceive your job. Follow our logic, and perhaps you will decide to follow our advice.

To begin, realize that your job is voluntary. In most of the world, indentured servitude and forced labor have been abolished. You are free to work or not to work, free to accept or reject a job. When the opportunity presents itself, you are free to start your own business (as one out of twenty people does each year), free to change jobs, and free to not work. You are free to work for free, free to retire from work, and free to drop out altogether. The actual responsibilities you have in life may not allow you to feel as if you have such freedom, but you do.

This freedom of choice—to stay or leave—plus the nature of the workplace today requires a change in the way you see yourself at work. In a labor market changed by technology, streamlined communications, new kinds of market demands, downsizing, mergers, and strategic alliances, loyalty still exists. But, like wild salmon, it is in danger of extinction!

It is time for you to see that your "real" boss is you. Whether you have other employees or only yourself, you are effectively your own small business, your own little company.

The "real" business: Company-You.
The "real" boss: you.
The "real" product or service: your labor, your ideas, your time.

The "real" customer: The people who buy your product.

Why the self-centeredness? Actually, it has always been there. All companies are buyers of labor. There was a time when companies defined themselves as their employees and when employees saw the company as "family," not a client, and expected to stay until retirement. No longer. Not in this labor market.

When you make this small shift—from thinking you work for someone else to becoming the proud owner of Company-You—a role reversal occurs. Once you are "boss" of Company-You, your "other" boss essentially becomes your customer, and you are in the business of serving that customer with the best work you can do.

The written or verbal agreement to employ you is virtually the purchase of your labor or the product of your labor. You agree to provide certain services, and your "customer" agrees to pay you for them at a certain price. Getting the job means you made the sale.

Read the business section of the newspaper and see how the economy is divided into two sectors—one consisting of service sector jobs, the other of manufacturing sector jobs. The Company-You approach makes this artificial divide between the manufacturing and service sectors irrelevant, because at Company-You, all work becomes service work. Everyone is selling a service, whether the "service" is running a machine, processing data, designing an ad, selling a product, bussing a table, processing a retail sale, teaching, or cleaning teeth. When you regard your work as your business—a personal service company—doing something for someone else that he or she wants done, this small change has profound consequences.

*It changes your attitude.* You begin to take pride in your independence and pride in your product.

*It gives you a fresh outlook.* The future takes on a different perspective, since forecasting is essential for every company, including yours.

*It affects your decisions.* It increases your responsibility for planning, growing, and protecting your business.

*It transforms your job interviews.* They become sales calls, and a job search becomes a marketing strategy.

With your new perspective on work as a personal service, Company-You needs to do what all good companies do on a regular basis—they write, review, and update the following.

*A code of ethics:* what you will and won't do

*A mission statement:* your goals

*A description of your products:* your skills; your resume

*A business plan:* your strategy for achieving your goals

*A company price list:* what your product is worth

When you review your company's business plan, consider these questions:

How can the quality of my product be improved?

How do my products compare to the competition?

Can I justify a price increase?

Should I offer a discount?

Should I look for a new customer (i.e., change jobs)?

Should I reposition my company or invest or gamble on providing a new service?

Indeed, when you see yourself as self-employed—no matter where you work or what you do—you will feel more control over your destiny, more pride in the work you do, and more incentive and confidence to move on to better opportunities. As all well-respected success stories demonstrate, when Company-You takes pride in its work; is fair, honest, and trustworthy; and can boast of excellence and deliver on time, greater success will almost always follow.

## Feeling Fresh at Work

Feeling fresh may be one of the biggest challenges of any work, especially if we work long stretches, in difficult conditions, or at demanding jobs. Those who work at home also face the challenge of feeling both mentally and physically fresh.

The changes we suggest in this section may not have the power to freshen you up after a sleepless night with a newborn or a hard night of partying. They can, though, keep you feeling as good as possible while you work. Here are some suggestions for small changes.

*Get enough sleep.* This is one of the best ways to feel fresh at work. Perhaps you need an hour or two more than you are already getting. (See page 77 if you are not.)

*Get fresh air whenever possible.* If you can, open your windows. When you can, go for a walk at lunchtime or during a break.

*Work in short spurts.* Take lots of minibreaks, stretching your arms, rolling your neck, or standing up and walking around if you work at a computer. If you stand on your feet a lot, sit down whenever you can, stretch your legs, massage your feet, and roll your neck.

*Try office yoga.* Do Bathroom Yoga (see page 51) when you take a restroom break, or try Larry's simple Workplace Yoga Routine at a desk, as follows.

**FORWARD BEND.** Move your chair two to three feet away from your desk. Place your hands or forearms on the desk. Stretch your spine back to your tailbone and look at the floor (see the illustration). If you want, press your abdomen against your thighs.

**BACKWARD BEND.** Press on the front of the desk and arch your back, gazing up at the wall or ceiling (see the illustration on page 196). Continue pulling your lower back in. A variation of this pose is to do it with your hands intertwined behind your head, pulling back on your elbows and shoulders.

**SPINAL TWIST.** Sit up straight and twist to the right, keeping your feet forward. Look over your right shoulder and twist. Now hook your right elbow over the back of your chair and pull. Your left hand can grab the right armrest or seat to help push you around. Repeat for the left side.

**SHOULDER RELEASE.** If you store a lot of stress in

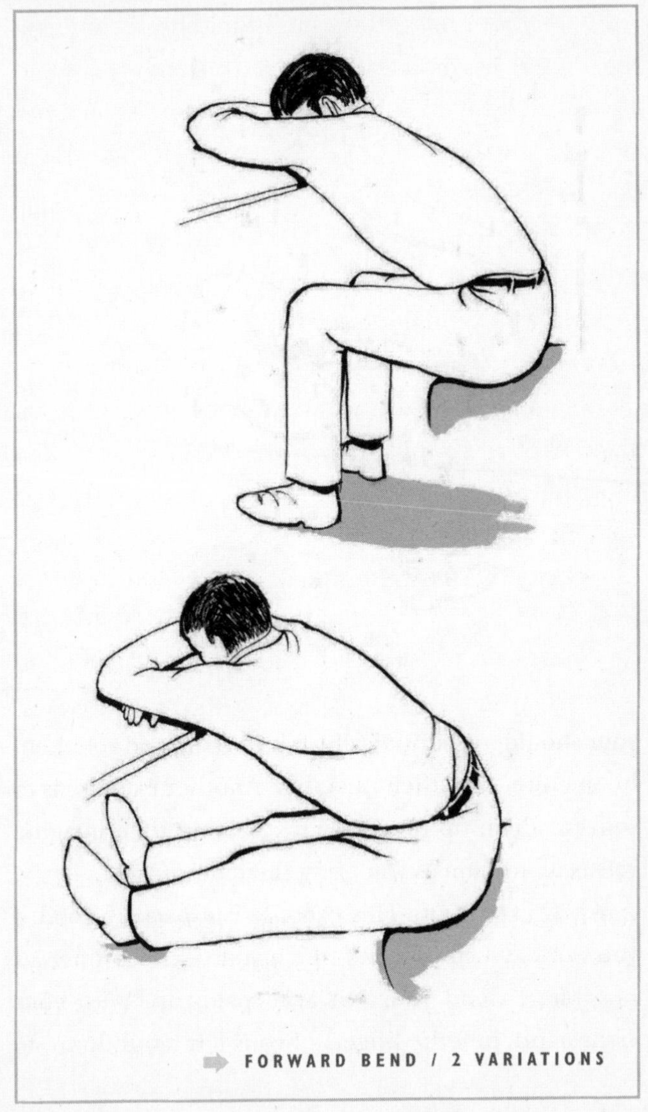

FORWARD BEND / 2 VARIATIONS

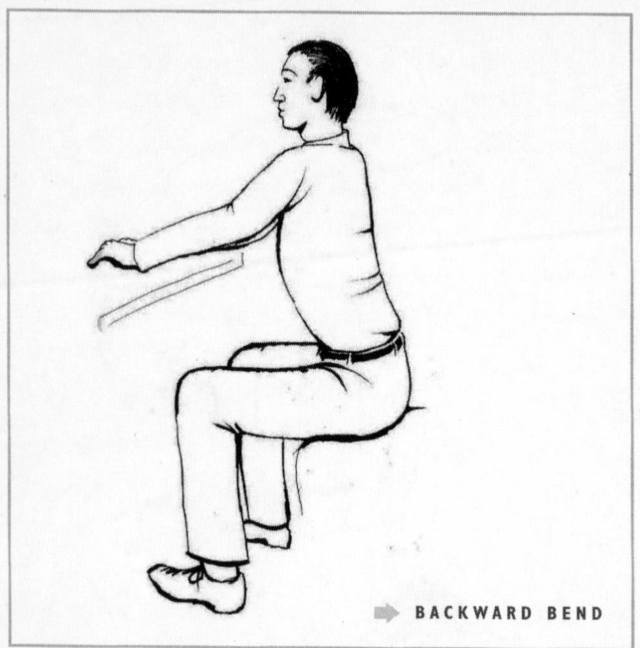

BACKWARD BEND

your shoulders, periodically stop working and roll them in one direction, then the other. Another exercise is to squeeze them up toward your ears, and then imagine releasing tension as you bring them down again.

**WRIST STRETCH.** This exercise is especially good if you work at a computer. Stretch your wrists as often as possible. Extend your left arm, palm up. With your right hand, pull the fingers of your left hand down, to stretch your hand into a back bend. If you want, use your right thumb for leverage. Repeat for the other hand.

Taking a few minutes to do any combination of these yoga stretches will go a long way toward relieving tension and keeping you fresh throughout the day.

*LSD (Low, Slow, Deep) Breathing.* Take ten low, slow, deep breaths to relax.

*Sit in a comfortable chair.* Be sure that your chair and desk are suitable for the work you do. If they aren't, adapt them or lobby for new ones.

*Massage your feet.* Keep a foot roller or massager under your desk. Stimulating your feet can rejuvenate your entire body.

*Change your shoes.* If you stand all day at your job, invest in good shoes. Change your shoes after lunch or later in the afternoon—this can give you a "second wind."

**HERE ARE SOME** ways to stay mentally fresh.

*Music.* Hum or whistle to yourself (aloud if you can). Or, if you have music at work, and it doesn't suit you, make a case for different music, offer to be in charge of the music, or wear earplugs—at least in one ear.

*Maintain a sense of humor.* Smile whenever you can. Laugh, too. Many people seem to forget their sense of humor at work—remember yours, and perhaps it will inspire others to remember theirs.

*Change your perspective.* Replace thinking "How am I going to survive until the end of my shift?" with "I only have to survive until the next break" (no more than a few hours) or "until things pick up" (any time).

*Stop watching the clock or glancing at your watch.* This does not make time pass any faster! If you are bored and it's okay with your boss, then cut out logic puzzles, riddles, and zen koans (Buddhist riddles such as "What is the sound of one hand clapping?") and use them whenever you are bored. (When you do have to concentrate, take a mini–mental break to stay fresh.)

*Break up the day into sections.* This is especially good if you get bored at work or if your work is repetitious. During each section give yourself a different topic to think about. On one you may think about your children, on another about your next vacation, still another your plans for the weekend.

*Take time off.* Sometimes the most important thing you can do to stay fresh at work is to get away from it. Enlightened employers understand this. Even if your time off from work is short, get in the habit of trying your best not to take work home or on a vacation. Make a total getaway, and you will be fresher when you return.

. . .

**THERE IS NO** magic elixir for feeling good at work, especially at a job you don't enjoy doing. Still, small changes can *improve* how you feel—physically and mentally—and thus make work less stressful and perhaps even more fun, interesting, and rewarding.

## Better All the Time

The business equivalent of small change can be found in a Japanese strategy called *kaizen* that encourages constant small improvements. According to *kaizen,* a business *not* constantly changing and improving is going to stagnate or drift backwards. *Kaizen* teaches us to make "getting better all the time" a constant. Now, this is nothing new to many people. To keep their licenses to practice medicine, law, or dentistry, to teach, or to be a therapist usually requires a minimum number of hours enrolled in continuing professional training. But everyone can benefit from education and more training. A business owner or executive can improve by making it a habit to visit similar workplaces, participate in professional development programs, or attend industrial fairs and conferences.

Management books and tapes are another great source for new ideas. Anyone can keep abreast by reading their industry's trade journals (and not just letting them pile up).

In addition to these traditional methods of improvement, there are small changes you can make. For example, to expand the menu at our local drugstore/ice-cream parlor, Mary Ann (who makes the best milkshakes in the world—really) added an electric frying grill to make grilled cheese sandwiches. It was a small improvement but much appreciated by the regular customers. Our daughter Marni's friend Brad improved the vegetarian burger at our local deli by merely adding grilled onions.

Get in the habit of looking for small ways to continually improve your job or business. Adding an employee suggestion box or putting aside an hour a week for employees to brainstorm small changes can make a big difference in the way they feel about their workplace. And if you are one of the employees, it can make a difference in the way you feel about your work.

Another small improvement is to shift your perspective from seeing what you do as a job to seeing it as a career. Invest in your future. If you work in the food service industry and like to cook, enroll in culinary classes. If you like gardening, study landscape design. If you like woodworking, learn how to design and market furniture. Study a foreign language or learn sign language to expand your employment opportunities.

Help others improve their skills. Our friend Leslie, the director of our community's public library, recognized that only a few of her staff had professional library degrees. Leslie searched for scholarships, grants, and other funding to pay for staff members to earn library science degrees. Now nearly half of her staff members have library science degrees—primarily because Leslie made staff development a priority.

Anyone can improve. If you are a receptionist, work on improving the quality of your voice, your speech, or the smile you greet coworkers with each morning. If you are shy, you can focus on ways to reduce your anxiety, gain confidence, and learn to make social contacts easier and more pleasurable. If you make presentations, join a group like Toastmasters to improve your public speaking skills. Or make a small change by taking a short course in communications.

And if you don't like your job at all, or want to move from a job to a career, take some time to research courses, educational programs, apprenticeships, or internships that will help you expand your choices. Our friend Stephanie, for example, worked at a clothing boutique but wanted to become a floral designer. She took the first step by working at a flower shop—one day a week.

Whether or not you ever have the opportunity to use what you learn, ongoing education is always beneficial. You grow more interesting, educated, and confident—and better prepared for any opportunity that comes your way. It may take years to become an overnight success, but if you never prepare for it, you'll wait forever.

## Ask More and Assume Less

There is no single formula for avoiding mistakes in the workplace. Nor is there one that can ensure success. There is, however, a single three-letter word that *minimizes* mistakes and maximizes your potential for success. We think this word is a great habit to acquire, especially in business. It is a sign of wisdom, diplomacy, and common sense.

This three-letter word can save you (and your employer or business) costly errors. It is easy to remember. We have even discussed it already (in relationships) but we want you to realize its broader applications. Here it is again: the three-letter word *ask.*

Ask where.

Ask why.

Ask how.

Ask for information.

Ask for knowledge.

Ask for guidance.

Ask to be sure, to be careful, to be right.

Ask if there is a better way, a better tool, a better system.

If you are in sales, ask for orders. If you are in collections, ask for money. It may go against all male evolutionary instincts, but you *can* ask for directions.

Ask for advice.

Ask for ideas.

Ask for help.

Ask your customers, colleagues, your boss.

Ask the person next to you on a plane, train, or bus.

Ask your friends, companion, spouse, or children.

To ask is not a sign of weakness—it is a sign of interest, motivation, caution, and conscientiousness.

Got "ask"? Here is the second part of the lesson.

Quiz time:

**Q.** What is the opposite of ask?

**A.** Assume.

**Q.** Why is it important not to make assumptions in business?

**A.** Because in the workplace, assumptions open you to much greater risk. They can lead to costly mistakes, unhappy bosses, disgruntled customers, and even tragedy, as the rising occurrence of medical malpractice cases stemming from faulty assumptions demonstrates. If the members of the medical team that performed a teenager's heart transplant surgery had not each assumed that the blood types had been checked by others, the patient might be alive today. And Larry conducted the funeral of a young man accidently killed by a wrong assumption made on a construction site.

Avoid mistakes by making this small change. *Ask more and assume less.* Replace assumptions with questions, and you replace a bad habit with a good one. Save the risks for your adventures—not for your job, career, business, future, or someone else's welfare. Maybe businesses should put an "Ask" sign next to the traditional "Think" reminder. There is enough risk in business.

One of the best small changes a business could make is to create a culture where *all* questions are encouraged. Sometimes what appears to be a dumb question contains the seed of a great idea. Sometimes it avoids a disaster. Larry's experience in manufacturing taught him that when the risks carry serious consequences (and even when they don't), it is always better to ask more and assume less, regardless of the question and how dumb you or anyone else may think it is.

## Seeing the Balance

Without balance, life would not exist. Consider the balance between our inhales and exhales, heartbeats and heart rests, waking and sleeping. Just as in our physical life, we need balance in our daily lives—between work and play, work and home, work and work. Work and work?! Larry's experience as president of a manufacturing company and later as its CEO taught him to recognize a unique balance: the balance between survival mode and opportunity mode.

Whenever resources are limited, the need to find balance arises. A teacher must find balance between fulfilling requirements (survival mode), and finding excitement in the classroom with new projects and learning styles (opportunity mode). Merchants and manufacturers need to balance their time and energy between meeting payroll, paying expenses, stocking inventory, and just staying afloat (survival mode), and finding ways to develop new products, new markets, and new ventures (opportunity mode).

Many kinds of work favor one mode over the other. An emergency room nurse, for example, works mostly in survival mode, while an industrial designer probably spends most of the time in opportunity mode.

If survival mode fills most of your day at work, why not take the month to find a way to spend more time in opportunity mode? If opportunity mode is your gangbuster approach to success (as it often is, by the way), use the month to make survival mode more efficient. Stop procrastinating about mundane tasks such as organizing your expenses, catching up on your correspondence, or reorganizing that disorganized filing system. This efficiency should give you more time for opportunity mode.

Understanding survival and opportunity modes helps you find the balance between what needs to be done (to survive) and what can be done to grow (opportunity). In your work, there is a time for each. Learning to find balance between limited resources, time, and energy presents a challenge to most people—especially the organizationally challenged among us!

(Larry suffers from this, especially when it comes to the mail.) The reward for improvement in this area of your life, however, is less frustration about what you can and cannot do—and perhaps you can find more time for doing what you like doing.

The small change to make is this. *Learn to be aware of the mode you are in,* as well as the mode your work requires of you—in general and from day to day and even hour to hour. Then strive to find a healthy balance between survival and opportunity. It might also help to remember our variation on a familiar prayer, which we call the Serenity Prayer for the Workplace:

Grant me the serenity to survive the things
  I must do . . .
The courage to pursue the opportunities
  I can . . .
And the wisdom to know the difference.
Amen.

## The ABCs of Managing Time

**QUIZ TIME, AGAIN.**

You are given three hundred colored paper clips and asked to sort them within three minutes. What method will you use? Choose from the following answers.

**1.** You grab a handful and start making a pile for each color. One by one, as quickly as possible, you put pink clips in the pink pile, red in the red pile, and so on. Then you grab another handful and continue until you finish or the three-minute time limit is called.

**2.** You search for all the red clips and put them in one pile, then find all the yellow ones and put them in a pile. There are two more colors, but sorting them is easier because there are only two colors left—unless of course your time runs out.

**3.** You make three piles. In pile 1 you put all the white clips (because white paper clips are your favorite—you like the way they blend in with the paper—you think they "say something" about your design sense). In pile 2 go the blue clips, because you hate the color blue and would use them only as a last resort. Pile 3 consists of all the clips left. (You are smiling, too, at how clever you think you are to think of this method.)

**4.** You take all the paper clips and divide them into several piles, with no system for sorting. (Who cares how many clips are in each pile or what color they are—you followed the rules, after all.)

**5.** You ignore everything and do something more important than sorting colored paper clips.

You guessed it; this quiz is a metaphor for work. At work, you often do exactly what is asked of you because that is what you were hired to do and why you are getting paid. Sometimes you do what is most expedient because you are working against a deadline. Sometimes you have the freedom or time or money to be as creative about your work as you want to be. Sometimes you make the decision to prioritize what to do. And sometimes, as in the last answer, you have more compelling things to do, such as take the day off to care for a sick child.

Actually, Susan *was* blowing off time sorting colored paper clips when the true meaning of Larry's ABCs of Time Management (which he has been trying to explain to her for nearly thirty-five years) came to her in a flash. In fact, her epiphany about time management appeared shortly after she grew melancholy thinking about a story she read suggesting that she probably has around 1,000 Saturdays left in her life—1,400 if she lives to be eighty-five. Time is precious, and it is always running out.

Turning to our ABCs of Time Management and the small change involved, you can use it to make better use of the time you have at work and even of the time you have in your life—and Susan can make better use of her Saturdays.

Here's how it works. Use a simple rating system to assign a grade—an A, B, or C—to *every*thing that needs to be prioritized.

**A:** Very, very important
**B:** Important
**C:** Not so important

To illustrate the ABCs of ABC Time Management, we'll use our friend Joe, who is a sales representative. As in most businesses, Joe has a few good accounts that are his "bread and butter," that account for approximately sixty percent of his income (which is true for many businesses.) Most of the rest are worth keeping because they generate income but nothing in comparison to the bread-and-butter accounts.

Joe needs to rate all of his customers.

**A LIST:** The few who provide the bulk of his business

**B LIST:** Those who supply small but regular business

**C LIST:** Those who once in a while place a small or modest-sized order

Now that Joe knows "Who's Who" on his three lists, he can prioritize his time and energy. Whom to call regularly? A list. Whom to call sometimes? B list. To whom to devote the greater portion of his entertainment allowance? A list (or potential A-listers). Whom to call for coffee? B list.

Joe arrives at the office after lunch to find five messages. Which customers will he call first? Now you know.

One caveat here. While ABC Time Management is a great strategy to use, there are exceptions. With time and attention you may be able to "upgrade" your customers—transform a B customer into an A customer and even upgrade a few of your C customers. The secret to success here is to be selective and to know that you cannot transform *all* of them, only some of them.

People who put too much time into the details of their work—details that belong on C lists, whether it be

C list customers, C list mail, or C list chores—are "micromanaging," and are so caught up in details that they fail to see the big picture.

People who don't know an A list from a C list are in danger of wasting time and energy (and losing a good customer).

In the A list areas of your life, you want the ABCs to show you how to do as good a job as possible, even strive for perfection. In the C areas, such as ironing every single wrinkle out of a garment, perfectionism is a *waste of time.*

On the other hand, you cannot put *all* your focus on A lists. B lists and C lists are still part of your life. If you neglect them completely, they can grow into big parts of your life—big problems, that is. Changing your car's oil, for example, may not be as important as filling up an empty gas tank, but it still counts for something and has to be taken care of eventually.

If you are in the habit of neglecting your C list, allocate some time for it, perhaps on a regular basis. Just don't spend too much time or energy trying to be a perfectionist.

**ABC MANAGEMENT** can be used in any area of your life that requires prioritizing.

*Your social life.* Invitations to two parties? Go to the party of the B-lister rather than that of the C-lister.

*E-mail.* This is a no-brainer. A list includes e-mails that require immediate response. B list is for when you would otherwise play a game of Spider or FreeCell. C list is the spam you ignore.

The beauty of ABC management is its simplicity and universality—it can be applied to all areas of your life: studying for an exam, shopping, budgeting, entertaining, and of course, work. Use it often, but keep it as a guideline, not a rigid rule.

**CLEARLY,** a small change that can make a big difference is to apply the ABCs to an area of your life where your time seems to slip away. Or start rating the items on your to-do lists, then put as little time and resources on C items as possible. Another change would be to stop shaping your entire life as one big to-do list.

Learning your ABCs was the first step to reading and writing. Learning the ABCs of Time Management could be the first step to finding the time to do what is most important to do—at work, at home, everywhere.

## Work to Home

You spend many hours at work—with its deadlines, pressure, crises, or boredom. Afterward, do you take the problems home with you? Are you cranky? Quick to anger? Impatient? Do you rely on alcohol, marijuana, or prescription drugs to help you go from work to home? Or do you keep your feelings bottled up, rely on passive-aggression, and wear your stoicism as a badge of honor?

Habits add up over your lifetime (as we have reminded you throughout this book!). Make the transition from work to home as smooth as possible and avoid damage to yourself and your relationships. Here are some small changes that can make the transition go more smoothly.

*Redefine commuting time as transition time.* If you drive, turn off the cell phone. (You will be a safer driver anyway.) Play good music and consider singing along . . . even aloud. If silence would serve you better, turn off the radio, forget about the news (it will be there when you get home), and gift yourself the silence. If you commute by train or other public transportation, use a portion of the time to daydream, meditate, or do LSD (low, slow, deep) breathing or deep relaxation.

*Make a deal.* If you carpool from work, help your companions to relax and lighten up (unless they prefer quiet time). A good laugh is a great antidote for fatigue and stress, so share those e-mail jokes or tell the funny stories you glean from work.

*Exercise.* Our daughter-in-law Alicia often walks home instead of taking the bus. As we write, she has traded her mountain bike for a road bike more suitable for peddling up and down those notorious San Francisco hills!

If exercising your way home isn't a choice, find a way to exercise immediately after work by taking a walk, running, aerobics, weight-lifting, swimming, yoga, or dancing. You gain the benefit of both the exercise and the release of tension.

*Make your arrival home more pleasant.* A routine as simple as kissing your companion, hugging your children, playing with your pet, or turning on your favorite station or CD is always a reliable transition.

Try "door therapy." Shift gears before you step over the threshold of your door. In fact, use the door itself to bring a smile to your face by posting on it your children's artwork, photos, or a memento from a vacation or party. Susan transformed the outside of our grungy garage door by plastering it with a cheerful patchwork of torn wallpaper samples. Next to the door she hung a poster of Yoko Ono and John Lennon embracing and another of Renoir's famous smooching couple. It's not a house-beautiful entryway, but it always brings a smile to our faces when we enter, and it serves as a clear reminder that our home is our haven.

Since we began working at home, in an empty nest, a few years ago, that threshold between work and home is practically nonexistent. But the passage from work to leisure is still important, especially since our work is always so visible. Sometimes we make the transition by leaving our home to eat dinner out or take in a movie. At home we shut the doors to our work areas.

*Relax.* Relaxing is one of the best ways to go from work to private time, especially when you work at home. Susan's mother, who was a busy homemaker, would (and still does) catnap before starting dinner. After a long day cleaning a college sorority house, our friend Annie Mae relied on a long bath for her relaxation. Other easy ways to relax include leisurely strolls or making a special phone call to an old friend. Better yet, meet a friend for afternoon tea.

Alcohol has always been a way to decompress, and while we don't encourage it, we see nothing wrong with having a glass of wine, beer, or a mixed drink if you want. Just beware of when one drink leads to many or if the time to decompress takes all night—or never comes.

*Have a ritual.* The nearly universal ritual of changing into clean, comfortable, at-home clothes helps create a peaceful mood, especially when along with your work clothes you imagine putting aside the workplace and any work-related stress.

You may want to engage in a religious ritual, alone or with others, giving thanks for the blessings of the day or praying for the strength to get through another day! Consider "handing over" to God the problems associated with your job or business.

**EVEN WHEN**, or especially when, you take work home to do later in the evening, transition-out for at least a few hours.

Finally, if your spouse works outside the home but you are at home, or off from work that day, attempt to honor his or her transition time, so your evening together can be more pleasant.

**ONCE YOU COMPLETE** the passage from work to home, *be home.* Or, as Thoreau's advice for being wholly present in the woods directs, be wholly present and don't allow yourself to be "back at the office." If you think people don't mind your distant nods or "What did you say?" questions, you're wrong. And the people in your life after work deserve more. You deserve more.

A healthy transition that allows you to be fully present at home, or wherever you go after work, will lead to a healthier, happier, more fulfilling future for your entire household—even if you live alone.

## Do You Like the Work You Do?

Are you happy at work? Do you like what you do? Do you think your friend's job is better than yours, your spouse's work more exciting, your neighbor's career more challenging, anyone's job more satisfying? If you loathe your job, want a new career, or wish you were working somewhere else but are nervous about making a *big* change, a small change can help you *slowly* improve your working life. Slowly. So don't hand in your resignation and wake up tomorrow thinking you have it made.

Some people have no idea what else they would do, or what they may be terrific at doing. Others know but, for practical reasons, are stuck in work that is just a job, ill suited to their temperaments, interests, talent, or other factors. Or the job they want is beyond their reach.

Our recommendation for a small change is to start with a call to a vocational counselor. Look for help in your situation; seek advice in preparing a résumé and looking for job-training programs or employment opportunities. Religious affiliated groups, such as Jewish Family Services, and other nonprofit organizations offer such services at low cost or for free. Many college alumni groups offer networking. Our friend Chloe, for example, found a job in Los Angeles through an alumni job network. So remember the magic word *ask.* Another option is to work with a book that helps you assess your own situation, such as *What Color Is Your Parachute?,* the classic vocational bible.

Does something else look appealing to you, but you don't know much about it? If, for example, being a nurse looks more appealing than your current job in retail sales, volunteer in a hospital and get an inside look at the medical world. Does journalism interest you more than teaching? Call a local reporter and ask to interview him or her about the job.

Read trade journals for the industry you are thinking about. Find them at a vocational school or large library or by asking people who work in that industry. Even better, see if there is a nearby trade conference, exhibition, or professional meeting you might be allowed to attend. Even those with high fees often allow guests to attend a few meetings before making a commitment to join. Network by asking everyone you know if they know someone who knows someone doing what you think you might want to do. (Networking is like that sentence—requiring persistence and following a trail.)

Be creative. When Susan wanted to learn about documentary filmmaking, she called the local high school and volunteered to start a film club. She joined the local film society and enrolled in a weekend course in filmmaking. Five years later (this is small, slow change, after all) she knew far more about the industry than when she began.

Have a special hobby or collection? Consider expanding it into a commercial enterprise or career, as numerous antique dealers, stamp and comic book collectors, floral designers, decorators, caterers, and fashion mavens have done. As we said before (page 146), think twice about this one, but if you're ready, go for it.

Find seminars, workshops, or short courses to take that will give you an inside look at a new vocation. Check with adult education programs at community centers, high schools, and local colleges and universities to see what they offer. Look through those trade journals mentioned earlier. Check out long-distance or online learning courses. Think twice, though, before you risk taking the fun out of a hobby.

As with any journey, you may find you feel like a stranger at first. You may also find a place that doesn't suit you. Instead of inspiring you to continue, a seminar or course may dissuade you. This can be very useful. When Larry thought he wanted to be a professor of philosophy, he started taking philosophy courses at a local university. He eventually completed a master's degree in philosophy and, in addition, benefited from a valuable lesson: a closer look at the profession alerted him to aspects of the career he found unappealing. Teaching no longer looked better than his career in business. Without the experience, he might always have second-guessed his decision to stay where he was.

If you like your work but would like to do it somewhere else, pick a day and begin devoting a little time each week to checking out other cities, companies, or industries where you might find a change of scenery.

Another option is to slowly work toward a career advancement or even a different career. Keep your job but enroll in a program that allows you to work toward your goal at your own pace. Susan's college roommate Kim trained as an artist but wanted to become an architect. For *ten years* she took one class at a time until she had earned a degree in architecture.

Another approach is to find yourself a mentor and volunteer to be an assistant. In this way you become an apprentice, learn new skills, and make new friends in a new business. This is how Chris became a librarian. First she volunteered at the library, then she was hired part-time, and eventually the library paid her tuition for an advanced degree in library science. Now she has a full-time job as a children's librarian.

Maybe you will never be happy in the workforce, as is some people's experience. Perhaps it is *outside of* work where you will gain the most satisfaction in your life. Many people have a passionate pursuit (see page 142) that they think about while working and do when they aren't working. Others devote time after work to nonprofit organizations or volunteer for worthy causes that give their life the fulfillment that their work does not always provide.

Perhaps the smallest change you can make when you don't like the work you do is to see your job in the larger context of your life: as a stepping-stone to a new job or career, as an incentive to advance your education or training, or as a means to allow you to do something extremely gratifying outside of work. Whatever you do, though, if you are unhappy with your work, do something. With patience and perseverance, even the smallest change will eventually take you down a different path—and make a big difference in your life.

## Add a Spiritual Dimension to Your Work

All the great religions in the world offer teachings about work. Judaism has much to say about business ethics, from prescribed rests for your work animals or land to the canceling of debts. Catholicism focuses on social justice issues, while the Protestant work ethic of hard work as praise for the Lord is deeply imbedded in our culture. The Quakers teach that work is a manifestation of love. Buddhists promote "right livelihood"—work that does not cause suffering. What these teachings have in common is the message to perceive the spiritual dimension of our work; to see work as a higher service—to our families, communities, all of humanity, all life on earth, future generations, and God.

Adding a spiritual dimension to your work means that both what you do and how you do it matters. Religions may differ on the particulars, even quarrel over them, but what they share in common is the value of service to others, and to God.

All teachings espouse some variation of the Golden Rule and its admonishment to treat others fairly. All teach the responsibility of looking out for others less fortunate than ourselves. And all encourage service to remove suffering.

Given the heavy demands of our work, it is easy to see ourselves as slaving away for a paycheck or a commission, or for our families, and thus failing to see the spiritual dimension of what we do (or ought to be doing). We may see religion or spirituality as a part of our life but something outside the context of our work.

Many jobs directly serve others in need—particularly jobs in the health and social service fields, in police, fire, and rescue services, and in the ministry. In other types of work, such as graphic design or retail trade, where often there is no obvious service, we may need to seek out ways to serve. It is especially easy to fall into the trap of thinking that if only we made more money we could afford to be more charitable.

Here is the change we recommend. Start looking for a higher service in your work, in addition to the service you may be selling. Look for the connection between your work and the lessening of someone's suffering. You can get in the habit of adding a dimension of giving at work by giving some of your time or talent to others who cannot otherwise afford it, whether it is pro bono work or giving away extra inventory. If you work in a grocery or bakery, arrange to have the day's leftovers taken to a shelter or to the homeless (or lobby management to do this). If you work in a restaurant, give food to the destitute when you can. One superb (and immaculately clean!) shelter in Akron began by serving such meals during the Great Depression and is still going strong.

If you work in retail or the garment industry, at the end of the season, arrange to make donations to a local women's shelter. If you have expertise in law, medicine, carpentry, or painting, you can make a habit of doing work for organizations, such as Habitat for Humanity or Doctors Without Borders, in need of your talent and expertise. You can also get in the habit of saying yes when asked to volunteer.

The Indian poet Rabindranath Tagore wrote: "Let me light my lamp, says the star, and never debate if it will help to remove the darkness." This applies to the assembly worker who can visualize the child who will read by the light of the lamp she assembles or the data processor who sees the value of stored information, the physician who donates time to vaccinate poor children, the employee who organizes a blood drive at work. *Any* job or workplace offers the potential to help others—or to paraphrase the Bible's advice to be charitable and to "give away part of the field."

**SEEING YOUR WORK** in a spiritual context has other implications. It helps you set a code of ethics or governing principles, then gives you the incentive to commit yourself to them at work. Words such as *honesty, integrity, compassion,* and *justice* belong as much at work as anywhere else in your life, not just because they help you stay out of trouble but because they are the right thing to do. Apply them in your decisions and fall back on them during your dilemmas and conflicts.

**NO DISCUSSION OF** a spiritual dimension of work is complete without raising the question of work as a calling. Doesn't the actual word "calling" imply a *call* from another dimension? Perhaps it is the call to use a specific talent or ability that you have had since childhood or developed during your life. Perhaps it is a duty you feel compelled to discharge, as those who inherit enormous estates or are part of a political dynasty may feel. Perhaps it is the way you choose to serve your higher power, as Mother Teresa served the poor, or the actor Paul Newman supports a special camp with the profits from his food products. Or perhaps it is a leadership role you feel driven to fulfill in the incredible tapestry of human life, as our son's friend Tom feels about his quest to enter the political arena, dreaming of becoming president of the United States.

When you begin to see the higher service in your

work, you will bring a spiritual dimension, understanding, appreciation, and code of ethics to what you do at work *every single day.*

# 6. Small Change for More Happiness

Every change suggested in this book, in every area we have looked at, has been designed to bring you greater happiness, satisfaction, security, and spiritual well-being. Good health is priceless, relationships provide comfort and security, work gives satisfaction, and creativity brings pride and fulfillment.

In this last chapter we offer practical, emotional, and

spiritual suggestions for small changes that can affect *all* areas of your life. Choose one and begin building a happier future.

## Smile More

Smiling is one of the easiest ways to add happiness to your life and the lives of the people you encounter. Smiling uses facial muscles that are linked to areas in the brain that produce feelings of well-being and joy. In this way, smiling may improve our dispositions. It also improves the way other people respond to us.

Before going to work each day, Joseph Charles stood on a street corner near his home in Oakland, California, to wave at passersby heading to work. "Keep smiling," he would yell; then, as he waved them on, he'd add "and have a good day." Joseph smiled to about 4,500 people each day—nearly 1.2 million smiles in a year and 36 million over three decades. Talk about spreading goodwill!

Smiles, like laughter, give your immune system a boost. As anyone who has ever responded to a smiling baby understands, sincere smiles have the power to make someone more likable, lovable, and desirable.

To understand how smiles affect our dispositions, consider what goes on in your body when you smile. By way of a nerve pathway, your brain sends a message to the zygomaticus—your "smile" muscle. One end of this muscle is attached to the corner of your mouth, the other to your cheekbone. When it receives the message to smile, this muscle pulls your mouth into a basic smile. Basic because there are other ways to smile, such as the Duschenne smile, named for the researcher who identified it.

The Duschenne smile uses both the mouth *and* eyes, mainly the lower eyelid muscle that causes those creases known as crow's-feet. More important, this same muscle gives the special sparkle that is present in a "megawatt" smile, that engaging, contagious smile. Translated: this superior smile will make you feel better than a basic smile and also give others an even better impression of you.

Now that you have the scoop on smiling, here are some small changes you might want to consider.

*Smile more often.* The more you smile, the more frequently you activate the specific area in the brain that creates happy feelings and good moods. Smiling frequently gives your smile muscles a good workout. With strong smile muscles, your face—even in a resting state—will carry a smiling look, which can affect your mood and give you a general sense of well-being without additional effort.

*Improve your smile.* To get the most out of a smile, learn to smile as expressively as possible, especially with your eyes. Many people do not or cannot voluntarily use their eye muscles when they smile, but with practice, most can learn this—a small change that will give you the contagious smile and sparkle associated with the most cheerful people. Doing this also makes for the smile that can affect your mood the most and cheer you up.

Adding other muscles, namely the ones around your mouth that expose your upper and lower teeth, can also increase your smile's wattage. If you want the smile of a vixen, then use the muscles around your nose to cause your nostrils to flare.

People who are self-conscious about wearing braces often stop exposing their teeth when they smile. The problem is that when the braces come off and their teeth look great, they continue the habit. If this describes you, abandon the stiff upper lip and start using all the muscles around your mouth. By the end of the month, you will have restored your smile to a natural, happier appearance.

*Do smile exercises.* You can strengthen those muscles by doing these isometric exercises a few times a day—anytime and anywhere.

Begin by locating the major smile muscles that connect your mouth to your cheekbones by, of course, smiling. Then, using four of your fingers, locate the muscles and feel their bulge. Hold these muscles tight for the count of five, then relax them. Do this a few more times.

Now concentrate on adding the eye muscles by squeezing the outside edges as you smile. It helps to do this in front of a mirror. Imagine isolating those muscles and holding them tight for the count of five, then relaxing them. Repeat this a few times.

When time permits, conclude your exercise session by making yourself chuckle, then laugh—as hard as you can. Larry teaches these exercises in yoga class, calling them *Smiling Pose* and *Laughing Pose.* In fact, he considers smiling one of the most important yoga poses you can do.

*Make a small change on your teeth.* Although cosmetic dental work can be time-consuming and costly, a small change can improve your smile. One change would be to utilize a whitening toothpaste, or to commit to cosmetic dental work on just your top front teeth or perhaps one single tooth that needs work. (On how to save up for this project, read on.)

*Smile even when you don't feel like smiling.* Forcing a smile causes a "response pattern activation" in the brain that will activate positive emotions. This may be a conditioned response, but the happy *feeling* it produces is real.

If you want to pick yourself up when you are down, or bring more happiness to your life in general, laugh more. Watch a comedy or go to a comedy club, read a joke book or humorous novel, or—one of the easiest pick-me-ups—choose to spend time and make friends with people who have a fabulous sense of humor. Their ability to make you laugh and feel good will have a strong positive effect on your disposition.

*Know when to smile.* To paraphrase Ecclesiastes—give yourself a time to smile and a time to not smile. Wise is the person who knows when to do each. If you are in the nervous habit of smiling, or even giggling or laughing, when it is inappropriate, practice biting your lip. To suppress an inappropriate giggle or laugh, breathe deeply and slowly. If you can, remove yourself from the scene altogether, as there is nothing worse than to be laughing hard when you shouldn't be laughing at all. (We think most of us have some good stories to tell about *that* challenge!)

Remember, whenever you want more happiness in

your life (and who doesn't?), smile more, and improve the smiling you do by working on your smile muscles and making sure you use your eyes when you smile. When you feel gloomy but it is appropriate to be feeling happy, force a smile or, better yet, a laugh. As the song and the research suggest, when you're smiling, the whole world will smile with you.

## Slow Down

Are you always in a hurry? Do you race to appointments? Rush to social engagements? Sprint to catch the train or plane?

Do you eat on the run? Get anxious in long lines, panic over traffic snarls, and hate red lights? Be honest: Do you like to drive fast?

Do you always seem to be dashing through the days, rushing the weeks, and speeding through life?

If you answer yes to most of these questions, perhaps your small change could be to *slow down* (because slowing down will make a difference in practically all areas of your life). In fact, take as long as you need to slow your pace and return to pre-every-nanosecond-counts time. After all, why be in a hurry to slow down when your goal is to stop being in a hurry? Slowing down:

Allows you to be more careful and lessens the chance of accidents
Removes much of the stress caused by hurrying and worrying about it
Makes you a safer driver
Helps you to be more patient with everyone
Gives you time to think before you speak, talk more slowly, and listen more carefully
Allows you to be more mindful
Makes you eat more slowly and allows you to enjoy your food
Enables you to rely less on fast and processed food and more on home-cooked meals and pleasant dining experiences
Allows you to entertain more easily and make your guests feel more welcome
Makes you feel as though you had more time to live life

Slowing down in a hurried world may feel as if you are swimming against the current. Give it time, though, and it can become a habit. Here are some small-change suggestions to help you slow down.

*Make the decision to slow down.* You won't slow down until you see the benefits of slowing down. Visualize what your life would be like if you took more time to do the things you already do. Consider the effect slowing down would have on yourself, your family, your friends, and the people you come in contact with each day.

*Remember to slow down.* Get in the habit of checking your "personal speed" by remembering to ask yourself what gear you are in—supersonic, fast, just right, too slow. (Yes, there is a happy medium here—*too* slow, and you risk missing appointments and deadlines and driving your fast-paced friends a little too crazy.)

*Turn down the volume or turn off the noise.* Loud music makes us feel like speeding. Turn it down or turn it off, and you will be better able to slow down. If you need music to relax, then start listening to relaxing music!

*Commit to doing less and saying no more.* One of the primary reasons we are hurrying through our lives (and we are as guilty as the rest) is that we do too much and say no too rarely. Learn to beware of "distant dinosaurs"—volunteering to do something that looks small in the distance but, when the time comes, looms large.

*Make one night or one day a slow day.* Get used to what it feels like to be slow one night. Talk slowly, drive slowly, do everything you do slowly. We slow down on Friday night, for example. Or slow down for one activity, perhaps making a conscious effort to slow down in the car. This would mean listening to tapes or soft music, and making use of red lights and stalled traffic to do things like your smile exercise, breathing exercise, or memorization exercise.

*Concentrate on your breathing.* As we have mentioned so often in this book, become aware of your breathing, taking low, slow, deep breaths. This kind of breathing helps you slow down your pace and your thoughts, lowers your blood pressure, and makes you feel more relaxed.

*Learn to meditate.* If you are in a hurry to learn how to meditate, jump back to page 175, but we advise slowing down and enjoying the rest of this section!

*Make better use of waiting time, and you won't mind waiting.* Standing in line, for example, is a great chance to chat, and can even change your life. In 1970, while waiting in line to get a visa for our honeymoon trip, Larry struck up a conversation with a woman going on a yoga retreat in Ceylon, now known as Sri Lanka. In those days such information was passed only by word of mouth. We joined her on the retreat with Swami Satchidananda and a few students, including the (late) singer Laura Nyro and Alice Coltrane, the widow of John Coltrane—an experience that deeply influenced our lives and forever changed them. Most lines don't multiply into such powerful effects, but all lines have the potential for a pleasant exchange when you are in slow gear and eager to make the most of your waiting time.

In earlier chapters of this book, we referred to the classic race between the tortoise and the hare, and the lesson that slow and easy wins the race. Perhaps this is a good place to remind you of that lesson and to consider why running the race through life may be most effective when you run in slow motion. Now, take as much time as you need to ponder that thought, before you don't-hurry through your next small change.

## Make Enough Enough

Just as there is "more than one way to skin a cat," there is more than one way to feel rich. Here are some of those ways. Earn a lot. Inherit money. Marry someone with money. Divorce someone with money. Win the lottery. Find and deliver a Most-Wanted Terrorist.

Here's another way: want less. Here's another way: be content with what you have. Here's still another way: buy less and save more. Make enough enough.

We cannot give you a plan for getting rich because,

well, frankly, we don't have one ourselves. Nor do we have a plan for getting "all you want" in life. Motivational gurus make their fortunes telling other people how to make a fortune. We applaud them. Go read them. Take their seminars. Give their advice a try.

Making enough enough is *far* easier said than done. In a society of consumption, where we earn much of our status from how much we spend on our lifestyle, simple living seems an unattainable ideal, worth striving for but not at all easy. In one of the bibles of simple living, in fact, the author recommends downsizing to a smaller house. Finding the room to store all the detritus of your life in a house you have already outgrown is difficult enough; clearly, downsizing to a smaller home may look appealing but requires a Herculean effort.

Here are some of our secrets and small-change suggestions. We worry about money six days a week, but on the seventh day, we make a habit of taking a break from our worries. We don't go shopping, and we don't pay bills. Instead, we play and have fun.

When you do go shopping to buy a few items for yourself, get in the habit of not using a cart. Just carry what you can in your arms. That way you are not tempted to try every item that catches your fancy or to buy more food than you need. And if you do, it won't be a whole lot more than you need—only a little more.

When you shop, stay focused. An elderly woman friend taught us: "If you are going to Baltimore, don't stop off in Washington." If you are shopping for shoes, for example, stay focused on shoes and do *not* allow yourself to wander into the dress department, giftware, or anywhere that takes you off track. This small change will give impulse buying less of an opportunity.

Whenever you can avoid using an ATM for withdrawals, try this small change: withdraw money or cash a check at the bank, and get it in as small a denomination as possible. A wad of fifty one-dollar bills looks, and therefore feels, like more money than two twenties and a ten. Remember the goal is not to *appear* wealthy in other people's eyes—it is to *feel* as though you have enough, in your own mind.

Another habit to get into when shopping is to give yourself the amount you think you can afford to spend. Write this amount on a pad of paper or an extra check register. Then deduct from its balance each time you purchase something. This way you are less likely to get caught spending more than you have.

Break the habit of reading magazines that focus on rich people or advertise goods that only the wealthy can afford.

Get in the habit of shopping at places and for items that can be returned if you change your mind when you get home. When you cannot resist the impulse to buy, you will still have the option of not keeping what you could not momentarily resist.

Get in the habit of shopping at smaller stores. There are fewer (note, there are still *some)* temptations to lure you into purchases you would not otherwise make. (This also supports local, small businesses and a more relaxed way of life.)

If you buy more when shopping with friends, start shopping alone and plan other activities to do with your friends. If you find you buy less with someone else in tow, then try to have another person with you when you shop.

Finally, when you are faced with serious money problems (and we can report from that place firsthand), try to put them aside at bedtime. Get in the habit of thinking of something in your life that is going well or of a person you admire, or of something you have seen or read that day of particular interest. Replacement thinking (replacing a worry with a positive thought) will not make your money problems vanish. It can, however, take you out of the habit of brooding about them and allowing them to grip your every waking thought and your dreams as well.

Understand that you are in good company. Mahatma Gandhi never made much money in his life, nor did Jesus. Mother Teresa died poor, as did Vincent van Gogh. Rosa Parks was known for her courage, not the cash in her pocket.

Getting rich is the American Dream, and who are we to take on that one? All we are saying is that while it may be the American Dream and the dream of others around the world, it isn't the *only* dream or the *only* measure of success. And truly understanding that broadens the dreamscape to let you make enough enough.

## Accept What You Cannot Change

This book has been about making small changes in your life. But here's something important to consider: there are some things you cannot change. You cannot change your basic disposition. If you have a serious nature, for example, you are not likely to become Little Ms. Sunshine.

What you can change, however, is your *perspective* on what you cannot change. Our shortened version of the Serenity Prayer is this: *Learn how to make molehills out of mountains.* Give yourself permission to sweep a few faults under the rug. Adopt realistic standards, to appreciate that less is more.

Religious wisdom says that the rich person is someone who is content with what he or she has. Study after study demonstrates that wealthy people are only slightly happier than those of us not in that club. If street people in Calcutta can report a surprising level of contentment with their lives, surely we can. There are exceptions—and these include those who have experienced severe tragedies, such as the sudden death of a loved one or being the victim of a heinous crime.

Take an honest look at yourself and what you lament in life. This simple verse guided Susan as a young girl:

For every problem under the sun
There is a solution
        or . . . there is none.
If there be one, try and find it.
If there be none, never mind it.

Some people require more creativity to find the solutions; others require more acceptance to reach the never-minding. Such insights may come as instant epiphanies, others after years of therapy. Most come from the wisdom of living (perhaps the reason that older people report more satisfaction with their lives than younger people do).

The task we face in finding happiness is twofold, therefore. On the one side is improving ourselves. On the other side is accepting what we cannot change.

One way to accept what you cannot change is to reason it out through whatever system of reasoning works for you (after all, it cannot be changed anyway). For many people, religion or faith helps them learn to accept what they cannot change. It's okay to get creative here, though. So if it makes you happy (and that is the goal, after all), then use astrology (the stars gave me this destiny), karma theory (what I deserve from the past), existentialism (who knows why?), or whatever else may give meaning to your life.

**GET IN THE** habit of focusing on people's good sides (including your own), even if you have to post a list of their qualities. (It helps to remember that no one is perfect.) Then get in the habit of looking at the list from time to time—or all the time!

Get in the habit of replacing bad thoughts with good ones. Instead of "I'm too fat," think "I've got a great personality."

Another way to deal with a shortcoming is through

humor. Stephen Douglas accused Abraham Lincoln of being two-faced. Lincoln retorted, "Do you think I would choose this face if I had another one?"

Still another method for accepting what you cannot change is to think of the advantages of your shortcomings. We met a man who was born without arms. He said that instead of shaking hands when introduced, he got more hugs than anyone else he knew. He was someone who clearly knew how to see a shortcoming as an asset.

ONE THING WE can never change is our past. What we can change, however, is the hold our past has on our lives.

Here's some good news. Scientific research has demonstrated that you can change your memories of the past *by learning to be more selective* about what you remember. We are not talking about serious tragedies and transgressions here but the everyday thoughts that often fill our memories. So get in the habit of choosing to remember the best parts. For example, if high school evokes memories of taunting and loneliness, change your focus to remembering a favorite teacher or great summer vacation. If thinking of a broken relationship always brings bitterness, think of when you first fell in love with that person or a special time you shared.

Pollyanna-ish, perhaps, but this is about getting in the habit of being happy and not staying in the habit of holding a grudge.

Here's more good news. Research shows that you can let go of the idea that the past (if you had an emotionally impoverished childhood, for example) determines your future (you are destined to be emotionally impoverished your entire life). It doesn't. Holding on to this outdated belief, however, can leave you trapped in despair and destroy your hope of a brighter future.

Want to let go of the blame (on others or yourself) for insults, wrongdoings, mistakes, missed opportunities, and other evidence of human foibles? Then get in the habit of using a statute of limitations for how long you will carry a grudge (which we discussed earlier, on page 89). Just to remind you: we recommend a few days for a minor transgression, longer for larger ones, but never forever, unless something is truly unforgivable. Even then, some people find peace through forgiveness, but we are not advocating sainthood here. Our method is about small change that offers big payoffs.

**SO HERE'S THE SHTICK** on accepting what you cannot change. Try to make acceptance a daily habit. Acquire acceptance through religion, philosophy, and inspirational stories. Acquire acceptance with humor. And with grace. Little by little, through small changes in your perspective, you will give both shortcomings and the past less power to subtract from your overall happiness in life. If all else fails, acquire the habit of selective amnesia. It's one area in life where forgetfulness pays big dividends.

## Save for Something Special

We want to offer you a small change that may be a relic from the past, from a time when people actually saved money in a jar or bank *before* buying something special. This contrasts to the current custom of buying it and then paying for it *afterward*—with a credit card or payment plan.

Perhaps you remember yourself or your parents saving for something special this way. If not, you can draw your inspiration from the mother in the wonderful movie *My Left Foot,* the true story of a disabled Irishman who learned to paint with his left foot. His mother saved for his wheelchair coin by coin and kept the savings stashed away in a jar.

That's the way it used to be—as people saved for a rainy day, a college education, or a vacation. This is how

Susan's Uncle Jer and Aunt Nom saved for their son's bar mitzvah—by putting their change in a huge jar and watching it add up over the years.

Why this small change when you can use a credit card?

*Because it adds meaning (and not debt!).* If you saved for months or years to buy something, the object will mean more to you than something that was easily acquired on credit. How you saved for it will always be an integral part of your enjoyment.

*You experience the anticipation, the fun, of looking forward to having that special something in the future.* Our neighbor says there are three keys to happiness. First, have someone to love. Second, have something meaningful to do. Third, have something to look forward to. Well, here is that third something.

Saving for something special is fun, but the practice also cultivates patience, offers teachings on delayed gratification, and reinforces the power and habit of saving itself. And it provides a wonderful example of responsibility and discipline that can be passed on to our children and grandchildren.

**NOW, LET'S** be honest. Some of us are already deep in credit card debt, and living from paycheck to paycheck leaves us little money for a "rainy day" savings account. Many financial experts suggest your "rainy day" fund should be equal to three to six months' income, in case you or the person supporting you loses the ability to earn a living. So instead of saving for that something special, why not save for the feeling of being "debt-free" or the security of having a sufficient "rainy day" fund?

Here are our suggestions for a saving plan, which you may want to adapt for yourself.

Decide on the purpose of your saving plan—something special, getting out of debt, or a rainy day fund.

Set an approximate financial goal.

Establish a place for your savings. If they exceed a few hundred dollars, then open a special savings account for your savings.

Give yourself a "tip jar" to collect the change and bills you save at the end of the day or week. Put a stack of savings deposit slips under it.

What goes in the tip jar? All your change at the end of the day or a set amount, such as five or ten dollars a week—whatever you can spare to save. All "found" money goes into the jar, so you might acquire the habit of looking down when you walk—you'd be surprised how many coins and even bills people drop and leave behind. (If you are superstitious, you have the added advantage of making wishes on these coins.) Your car or sofa may provide fertile ground in this area, so don't forget to look there. Any monetary gift or money you get from returning gifts goes into this savings, as does all or a portion of the "pin money" you earn from a hobby or selling part of a collection.

Whenever the jar fills or you think you have at least twenty dollars, make a bank deposit into your special account. If you receive money as a gift, make a deposit to this account. Did you get a bonus, tax refund, or other money you don't absolutely need for basic living expenses? Put at least a portion of it into your savings.

You may want to stash your savings in a secret hiding place (which is part of the fun) somewhere in your home. You will be less tempted to raid your savings, however, when you get in the habit of depositing it into a bank account and watching that account add up.

What did we save through this method? We used a special savings account to save for our son Dave's high school graduation present—a video camera. Because we had recently lost our major source of income—a family manufacturing business—we could not afford to buy the camera when he graduated. It took several years to save for it, but as we write this, he has enough money to purchase one. Over the years, Dave was tempted to spend his gift money on something else, but we always encouraged him to put most of it into his savings account. Now, besides the camera he is going to purchase soon, he has the added gift of a lifelong lesson—that small change adds up to something special.

AS WE HAVE said throughout this book, small change adds up. With this change you can literally see it add up. In some chapters, small change is used as a metaphor. In this section we mean it literally. Use it to add something special to your life, and use its teaching to give you the power and perspective to make the other changes you choose that much more meaningful and special as well.

## Advice for Slobs

Even if you have a high tolerance for chaos, do you really expect to find inner peace living in a disaster zone? Trust us when we say that our house *never* looks ready for a house and garden tour. We have a basic standard, which is that it looks and feels like home to us and is not revolting to others. To maintain a sense of inner peace, we have learned some useful habits (habits we wish we could have passed on to our children—while they were still living with us). If you would like to purge the slob within, here are some suggestions. May we remind you, though, this section contains *numerous* small changes—choose one small change, and choose to change yourself, not someone else.

*Make your bed every morning.* This is one of the quickest ways to gain a sense of order in your home. The rule requires a leap of faith, since it seems counterintuitive to spend time making a bed you will unmake only twelve or so hours later. In a messy home, though, a tidy bed is an oasis of order. That's all, and that's why, and that's that.

*All clothes and towels stay off the floor.* To someone inherently neat, this rule of conduct is self-evident. To a slob, it must be cultivated through much diligence and, again, requires a leap of faith. Letting the floor pile up with clutter creates living-space chaos more quickly than just about any other habit. Keeping stuff off the floor is easy to remember with the following "holding system." It has two basic components:

1. **THE CLEAN CATCHALL.** Use a clothes tree, open shelves, a big chair, or a series of large wall hooks on which to put the clean clothes you don't want to put away in the closet or drawer, where they "belong."

2. **A DIRTY CLOTHES CONTAINER.** Find an attractive container large enough to hold all the dirty clothes you accumulate between laundry sessions. This should be open and accessible. This system requires just two simple rules.

**RULE 1.** All clean clothes go off the floor and onto a clean-clothes holder—as soon as you take them off.

**RULE 2.** All dirty clothes go into the other container.

Could this system be *any* easier? Really?

*Start a discard plan and giveaway zone.* Conclude all major shopping sprees with a buy-one-give-one-away exchange. For every item you bought, discard one—into your giveaway zone. This can be a shelf, a shopping bag, a basket, or, if you want to get creative, a vintage suitcase. As soon as the zone is full, give the discards to a thrift store or homeless shelter, deposit them in a Goodwill bin, or arrange to have them picked up. Now start over again. This system works best when it is ongoing.

Quiz time: What do food, pharmaceuticals, and clothes have in common? Answer: A shelf-life. Whenever the shelf-life of an item is over—when it is out of style, worn out, or no longer works for you—purge, purge, purge. Do this as soon as you discover that the shelf-life is over, or do it at the beginning of each month or season. But do it!

*Become a wardrobe warrior.* Since your closets are unlikely to expand but the contents are, learn to be a wardrobe warrior. This requires *being honest with yourself.* If you try something on and decide not to wear it because you no longer like it, fit into it, or want it, toss it—into your giveaway zone. Have trouble making these decisions? In tough spots, follow this maxim. *When in doubt, throw it out, give it away, or tag it with a message about its meaning to you and store it in your attic.*

Dedicate a month to organizing your storage, then begin to purge and exchange. Once every five years or if you move, attack the attic—like a warrior, of course.

**TOO BUSY TO** clean? Too lazy to clean? Too tired to clean? Consider this: you can probably save enough money by packing your lunch or eating dinner out less often to afford a professional cleaning service every other week. Give up your daily designer coffee, and you can probably afford help at least once a month. If this doesn't work for you, consider one (remember—just one change at a time) of the following pick-a-day routines. (As in you pick the day, then stick with the routine.)

*Change the Linen Routine.* Each Tuesday (or another day of your choosing), change the pillowcases. Put out clean towels, bath mats, and dishrag or sponge. Whenever someone in your household is sick, change these daily. (Yeah, that's a pain, but so is spreading germs.)

No (and at the risk of grossing a few people out), we

are not going to tell you when to change your sheets. This method of cleaning is for *slobs.* It is about *small change.* To a slob, changing the bed can seem like a big deal, not a small change.

*The Trash Routine.* First, make sure that your trash receptacles can hold a week's worth of your trash. Then, on Mondays or Fridays (Mondays make it clean for the week; Fridays for the weekend)—even if it isn't your trash pickup day, and even if the wastebaskets are not full—empty all trash holders and put the contents in your trash receptacle. Ditto for the recycling bin in your kitchen or mudroom. Trash adds up quickly, and this once-a-week, no-nonsense routine keeps it manageable.

*The Sanitation Routine.* On the day when you don't have another chore, quickly (this is the key to success here), using a disinfectant, clean the sinks, countertops, toilet, bathroom mirror, and bathroom floor.

*The Rotation Routine.* This is actually a monthly cycle of routines:

**WEEK 1:** Pick a day to clean the shower or bathtub.

**WEEK 2:** Pick a day to do the floors.

**WEEK 3:** Pick a day to dust.

**WEEK 4:** Pick a day to do one of these routines again—just one.

Keep in mind that we are talking minimum maintenance mode. If you ever graduate to upper levels or hire a professional to clean for you, you won't need these simple routines anymore. Meanwhile, hang in there. They work. The secret to their success is that spreading out your household chores but sticking to a regular routine makes them easy to remember and easier to do and provides less excuses not to clean.

**HERE ARE A** few more suggestions, but again, remember to only choose one change at a time.

*Dirty Dish Dogma.* Never, we repeat, never, allow your dirty dishes to remain overnight in any place but the kitchen. Not in the dining, living, or family rooms, and especially not in your bedroom.

*Mail Mores.* Be ruthless and religious about incoming mail. This is based on the old proverb "A place for everything, and everything in its place." Delegate a place for incoming mail. One place. No other place will do.

As you sort the mail, put bills and correspondence in their proper places: always the same place, never with anything else. Keep this simple.

Display all invitations—personal and public—and appointment reminders on a bulletin board next to the phone, on a cabinet near your refrigerator or sink, or on the door you use whenever you leave home. Nothing else is displayed with them. Nothing.

Put magazines and catalogs where you do your casual reading.

Ruthlessly discard *everything else* except solicitations for donations you want to make within that month. These go with your bills.

**HERE'S A RULE** Larry's dad, Maury, tried (and failed) to teach him but we think merits mention. *A project is not complete until you have cleaned up after yourself.*

And another one Maury tried (and failed) to teach Larry. *Fix anything as soon as it breaks. If it can't be fixed, get rid of it right away.*

**ON A FINAL** note, if the price you pay for a clean house is constantly nagging others in it to live up to your standards, perhaps a small change you might want to make is this. Gift each person with a place to be themselves, and let go of your standards there. For instance, we gave our son Ari the area around his bed, which we defined with masking tape. Anything within the tape was his territory to trash as he pleased, the only caveat being not to leave any organic matter, such as leftover food, that could attract small living creatures. His wife now gifts him the same area, so there must be a deep pattern here.

. . .

**IF YOU ARE** used to living in clutter, you probably have the patience or ability to overlook things and let the improvement come slowly. Still, when you commit to purging the slob within and set your sights on cleaning up your space, be patient. It takes years and numerous small changes to reform a slob and make over a messy home. On the other hand, if you embark on this course in order to make living with a Type-A, cleaner-than-thou housemate possible, well, you might want to give that skip-or-pack-a-lunch-for-professional-cleanup-savings plan a green light. You are probably going to need it.

## Walk Your Talk

Let's get serious now (because we want to discuss a core aspect of character, and character is a serious matter). Are you dependable, trustworthy, honest, and responsible? To put it more simply but no less seriously: Can you be *counted on* to *do* what you say you are going to do? Or to put it even more simply: Do you walk your talk?

When you are in the habit of delivering what you promise, others learn to see you as dependable and honest. Yet there is a twist here, which is the habit of saying yes when you should be saying no. Often, when someone asks a favor, they catch us off guard. And being the nice people that most of us are, we don't want to let them down. The small change you might start is to teach yourself *how* to say no—sometimes.

Susan, being outgoing, altruistic, and enthusiastic, has the well-meaning habit of *volunteering* for tasks that are not big but still take time and are rarely *necessary*. For example, she'll offer to send an interesting article to someone. This means she has to take time to hunt for it through her extensive files, then take it somewhere to be copied, write a note, and mail it. A nice deed, but instead of verbally volunteering, she might get in the habit of making a mental note—to *herself*—then acting on it if and when she has the time. That way there is no commitment and no disappointment, and a nice surprise for the recipient when she follows through on her unannounced intention. When she volunteers and doesn't deliver, she gets upset with herself, since she knows she has been less trustworthy than she set out to be. The small change here: *end the habit of promising more than you can deliver.* Occasionally resist the urge to extend yourself beyond your reach. Again, learn when and how to say no.

Just as important as setting boundaries is this: *learn*

*when to say yes*. Our basic formula for when to say yes was inspired by a prayer, but you can develop your own. We say:

Yes to viewings and funerals.
Yes to visiting the sick.
Yes to all weddings and milestone parties (unless it is absolutely out of our budget or if there is a *major* conflict in our schedule).

We also say yes to just about any requests from our parents, a rabbi or minister, church or temple, and friends in distress.

Another yes we adopted is to each other. Marriage is a commitment to say yes, as much as possible, to your partner. Yes to requests for kindness and understanding, yes to invitations for comfort and support, yes to love and physical intimacy.

These are our guidelines; we trust that you can come up with your own. Formulate your list of yes occasions; perhaps discuss it with your partner; then post it somewhere as a reminder. Be clear on your priorities, honor them, and walk your talk.

**WHILE WE ARE** talking about social contracts, may we suggest a small change that involves trust. The issue is punctuality. Here again, we are a mixed marriage. Larry runs "on time" while Susan likes to leave "early" to ensure herself buffer time to guarantee being on time. Ask and try to understand how your friends and family feel about punctuality. When you make an effort to honor their feelings, you will earn their trust.

Often hard feelings, misunderstandings, unspoken disagreements, and angry incidents arise between partners and among friends and family over punctuality or lack thereof. If this is your issue, try to get a grip on it by calmly discussing the topic in general, not in the heat of the moment. Clarify under what circumstances each person's rules will apply, such as for movies, airplanes, parties, and appointments. Then honor your agreements.

Speaking of time, are you in the habit of going to social engagements late and leaving early—even slipping out without saying good-bye? First, we suggest the Golden Rule here. *Go when you would want others to come to your affair, and leave when you would want others to leave yours.* We base this decision on our take on philosopher Immanuel Kant's categorical imperative. We ask what would happen if everyone did as we want to do. For example, what would happen if everyone left the party early? Sure, you may have a valid excuse for leaving early, or think it is better to leave early than not come at all. Remember, though, that character is usually judged by what you do, not by how you reason doing it.

**TO PARAPHRASE CONFUCIUS:** "People's natures are alike; it is their habits that carry them far apart." If you care what others think of you, and care about others, if you want to be happier and make others happier, then walk your talk. Stop promising more than you can deliver and deliver what you promise. Strive to be on time. Work on just one of these, and you will be walking that much taller.

## See Yourself as a Teacher

Eat, drink, and be merry, the saying goes. This is one way to make yourself happy. Sensory pleasures, however, are not the same as satisfaction and, in our opinion, not as rich, though we love to have fun. Rather, one of the surest pathways to happiness and satisfaction with life is altruism—giving of yourself to others. And one of the most richly rewarding and natural ways to be altruistic is to teach someone something. Larry loves to quote the familiar adage *To give is to receive,* because to pass on knowledge or skills is to receive respect and validation.

Teaching can be as simple as sharing a family recipe. Keep your cookie recipe a secret if you plan to be the next Mrs. Field, but if you don't, why not spread happiness by sharing your favorite recipes? In fact, share whatever you know, whether you have a gift for music, painting, sewing, gardening, or collecting unusual artifacts.

Susan taught her mother, Debbie, to do needlepoint and to paint furniture. Debbie taught Susan how to knit and sew. Susan's father, Sidney, taught her to love history, especially local and family history.

We teach our children. We teach our children's children. We can teach other people's children. Being a Big Brother or Big Sister, for example, or mentoring someone who comes from a troubled home or whose parents are too busy to teach them, can be immensely rewarding. "Adopt" a niece and teach her the family recipes, how to knit, or how to play golf.

What you teach can become a legacy. Every Passover, as soon as the Seder dinner was complete, our uncle Jer taught his grandchildren, nieces, and nephews, all of whom are now in their teens and twenties, how to play every poker game that ever existed! When our eldest child got married, one of the highlights of the weekend was the family poker game—presided over by Uncle Jer and played until 3:30 a.m.! (Our son Dave won the evening's kitty, a win that meant more to him than just about any prize he has ever won.)

**GIVING SOMEONE** else the opportunity to teach you may be a blessing, especially for people who are housebound or unused to attention. When Susan wanted to study poetry and had a baby and a toddler, she asked the librarian to recommend a teacher and was given the name of a retired English professor who was caring for his housebound wife. He was as delighted with their Tuesday morning poetry sessions as was Susan. Each week she brought him flowers, homebaked bread, and new poems; each week he taught her how to shape her words and thoughts into poetry.

Larry's dad taught him as much about running a manufacturing plant as Larry had learned from his MBA at Cornell—and maybe more. Maury taught Larry how to lead by teaching (not scolding or threatening), how to set a good example, how to value quality, and how to do what is right, in business and in life.

**EVEN WHEN** he was traveling around the world on business, Larry made time to teach yoga and meditation.

Over thirty years later, he is still teaching—and still finding satisfaction. In fact, it is his insight and his teaching over the years that is the foundation for this book on small change.

You can be a teacher, too. All it takes is a willingness to share what you know, the patience to explain it clearly, and the humility to offer it unconditionally. And as the best teachers know, teaching teaches the teacher as much as the student. What a great deal.

## Pick a Day and Pick a Time

Our son-in-law Jason works long hours as a young lawyer for a city prosecutor. During the weekend, Jason loves to kayak. The tranquility of being so far removed from the noise and rush of his weekday life rejuvenates his spirit, and the excitement of the sport gives him something to look forward to all week. While he is committed to and challenged by his work, Jason's weekend play days are the highlight of his week. Even when you love your job or career, play time gives your life a healthy balance, a retreat from responsibility, a happy time to enjoy living.

Susan grew up in a small town, where on Wednesday

afternoons most professionals—especially doctors and dentists, and many merchants and businesspeople—took time off. Wednesdays were often known as "golf day" and as a day when cinemas and theaters offered special Wednesday matinees. Our friend Katie, who owns a boutique in town, doesn't close her store but carries on the tradition. Wednesday is her day off, and on Wednesdays she goes to the art museum or library, the knitting shop, takes a yoga or Pilates class, does a craft project, gardens, or does nothing.

Our daughter-in-law Alicia, who works as a client manager at a design firm, had allowed errands to erode her weekends. In order to restore Sunday to being a day of rest and play, she enlisted Ari's help, and together they devote an extra 15 to 20 minutes daily to doing the chores they normally did on the weekend. Only now they do them faster and more efficiently. The system proved so successful, in fact, that now Alicia manages to keep most Saturdays free for leisure, as well.

Do you have a regular play day? Improve your life by picking a day and then getting in the habit of playing on that day—doing anything your heart desires, because that is what children do when they play.

At this point, many of you may be shaking your heads and saying that we are out on limb, suggesting an *entire day* for playing, when you have work and activities that hardly give you five minutes to relax, let alone part or all of a day or evening. Stay with us on this one, because it is important. Small change requires patience—it can take months or even years to reach the goal of a complete day. So again, pick a day. Pick your form of play, and either keep the day to yourself or find someone to join you—this can change from week to week, of course.

*Pick your day.* Circle it on your calendar and even announce it to your family and friends. Once you set the process in motion, you will slowly begin making other changes. For example, if you have young children, arrange to have someone in the family watch them, hire a babysitter, join (or start) a babysitting cooperative, or trade with a friend. If your friend doesn't have children, offer help with tax returns or homemade soup in exchange for babysitting.

Next, schedule for pleasurable activities—or leave the day free—and commit only to the most essential errands or appointments on that day. Now, don't take this to an extreme, such as refusing to go to a wedding or another important affair because it conflicts with your chosen day. (Yes, we know someone who did this—to us!)

Your "pick-a-day" is a good day to take a class or

lessons, such as piano, singing, or dance, or to play chess, golf, or bingo. It is a good day for your standing date (see page 92). Setting aside a particular day makes it easier to set boundaries to protect it. Eventually the changes you make will add up—perhaps slowly—to give you a wonderful time for doing exactly what you want.

**JUST AS IMPORTANT** as play time, and perhaps even more, is time for spiritual renewal and growth. You can combine it with your play day or make it a separate day or time. For many people, Sundays is their day for this. In the morning they attend religious services, discussion groups, or classes or retreat to a place of spiritual renewal, and on Sunday afternoon and evening they socialize, relax, or engage in a favorite activity. On that day you can read spiritually inspiring books, meditate, or practice yoga longer than usual, as our daughter Marni does. Your day of spiritual renewal can also include volunteering for a worthy cause, from working in a soup kitchen to babysitting for new parents in need of a night out, as we have begun to do on Sunday evenings for the children of our friends and the friends of our children.

Instead of having one dedicated period during the week, many people commit some time every morning.

Muslims commit to prayer five times a day. Committing to a regular time each day or week makes it easier for you to say no to other activities that might prevent you from honoring your spiritual commitment to yourself.

For us, Friday evening, the beginning of the Sabbath, has become our regular time for spiritual renewal. Even though it was observed in our families, it has taken us a few years to reestablish this sacred time. Some Friday evenings we attend religious services, on others we stay home and relax or entertain friends. Occasionally we attend our local theater or go to the cinema or hang out at a bookstore or coffeeshop. Because it is a time for spiritual renewal, Susan refuses to watch body-count movies on Friday nights. (Saturday night is a different story. She will watch them, with the understanding that the next movie will be a slow-moving love story or an art film.) What we try to remember is to keep Friday evening reserved for spiritual renewal, not work, or chores—or anything that feels like punishment!

Clearly, more religiously observant people abide by more orthodox rules regarding their spiritual renewal. Again, though, this book is about self-improvement through small changes, not about radical makeovers or making over someone else according to your rules. Making time for spiritual renewal is important; how you make that time is your choice.

. . .

**PICKING A DAY** gives you the opportunity to establish play time and spiritual renewal as a dependable part of your week. In the past (and for many religions), those days were often set in stone. Pick a day, any day, but keep that appointment with yourself a regular routine—a day to enjoy, to remember, to look forward to—and to watch these days become some of the best days of your life.

## Count Your Blessings

People who are happy live longer. People who are happy live healthier lives. People who are happy are, well, happy. Here is one of the easiest ways to increase your joy, happiness, and life satisfaction. *Increase your gratitude about what is right in your life.*

Easy? Yup, as easy as counting, because what you do is count your blessings. Literally *count* them (this is as concrete as you can get). And this is habit-forming, because you are going to get in the habit of counting them on a daily basis. This is a small change that will yield big results over time.

In a small spiral notebook, write down at least three things from the previous twenty-four hours for which you are grateful. This can be as basic as "I am grateful for being alive" to "I am grateful for the fellow on the train who smiled at me even though I was having a bad hair, bad body, bad face, and bad dress day." You can get more universal and less self-absorbed—for example: "I am grateful to live in a democratic, pluralistic society." It doesn't matter what you think of, as long as you are grateful for at least three things that are going right in your life.

If you are having trouble thinking of what to be grateful for, then think about the bad things that *could* have happened to you—and didn't. Remember bad stuff from history, bad stuff from the news, from the weather, from the economy. Try not to dwell on bad stuff that has happened to you in the past, as it is better to think of bad stuff that has happened to someone else. (Thinking of the bad stuff that has happened to you doesn't allow you to let go of it, and that becomes an obstacle to happiness.)

Get in the habit of setting aside a few minutes each day—perhaps after watching the evening news or before you go to sleep, when you wake up, or when you are taking a coffee or lunch break—to count your blessings. It doesn't matter when you do this; it only matters that you get in the habit of doing it. It is also important to remember that this habit needs to be written. It is not a meditation or a prayer—it is a list. Over time, as the pages in your spiral notebook fill, you will have a growing, physical reminder of how blessed you really are. Sustain the habit over your lifetime, and you (and your family) will have volumes on what was special and good about your life.

Another approach is to make this small change with someone else. Again, set aside a time each day or each weekend—always the same time (this is a habit, after all)—for counting your blessings. It might be at a meal you always share. If this evokes a Norman Rockwell image of people gathered around the table praying, we remind you of this: the people in his paintings look happy!

In our home, we have a weekly ritual of lighting candles on Friday night to welcome the Sabbath. Afterward, with whomever is in our midst (sometimes our son and his friends getting ready to party at our house, for which we silently said an extra prayer!), we take turns telling something good that happened to us during the previous week or something for which we are grateful. A few people have trouble finding a single positive thing to say, which is easy to understand after a particularly bad week. But there is *always* something for which to be grateful, and that is the point here—to find it and to express it.

Now that our children are grown and gone from

home, we still keep up the tradition, as a way to count our blessings and as a way to remember the happy times we had raising our children.

**DO YOU** *really* want to change your outlook on life? Then break the habit of whining—that chronic complaining that is called "kvetching" in Yiddish.

Whiners tend to focus—and we mean *focus,* as if there were nothing else to think about or talk about—on what is not right in their lives. Familiar? The woman getting a divorce who complains about her ex—*every time* you ask how she is doing. How to stay stuck in one place! As this example shows, whining keeps you locked in your place of misery and bores the living daylights out of everyone else. Chronic complaining creates a perspective where you tend to overlook what *is right* about your life.

To stop whining and get back on a positive track, *try to actually solve your problem.* If you suffer from insomnia, start meditating or medicating. (Okay, see a doctor, sleep counselor, or therapist for help with this.) If you think you don't earn enough money, look for ways to spend less or earn more, or let go of it altogether.

If that doesn't work, try Replacement Therapy. *Replace your complaints with your list of blessings about what is right in your life.* If you are complaining about your spouse not doing the dishes, replace those complaints with what is good about him or her: his ability to dance well or to remember your birthday. If you can't think of one good thing to say about that spouse, perhaps you should replace the spouse.

*Replace your complaining with taking note of what is not going wrong in your life.* You are not waking up in a hut in a remote mountain village with no running water. If it is hot and you have no air conditioning, remember that you are not shivering through a winter in the frozen tundra.

So if you want to enjoy your life more and complain less, count your blessings. Three a day. Every day. This small change will change everything. We promise.

## Find Your Way

Remember our transcontinental pilot? The one who began flying slightly off course? The one who would have landed in the wrong country because of a one-degree error in navigation? As we have shown throughout this book, navigating through life is the same. With a reliable *moral compass*—an ethical code of conduct you choose to follow—you can steady yourselves during turbulent times, find your way when lost, and chart a course of goodness. To travel through life with no compass at all is to risk bobbing around, going nowhere special, or counting on luck alone to find your way.

What is your moral compass? Is it written out and posted where you refer to it regularly and can recall its wisdom whenever you need it? If you don't have a particular moral compass or if you have one but not on display, this could be one of the best small changes you can do for yourself.

All the great religions, philosophies, and cultures contain timeless wisdom and moral guidance that are as relevant in today's complex world as they were in yesterday's simpler societies. Often the moral code is a divine commandment or rule to respect and obey. Throughout history, many have struggled to follow them exactly, while others struggle to interpret them anew. For those of you, like ourselves, who seek greater understanding and less orthodox interpretation of the Ten Commandments, the Golden Rule, and other moral compasses, Larry offers his perspective—his Terkel twist, if you will. See the Ten Commandments as Ten *Commitments*; see the Golden Rule as a Golden *Commitment*. This perspective both gives you freedom and moral agency and keeps the responsibility for your behavior where it belongs—on your own shoulders.

In our home the Ten Commandments (oops, Commitments) are posted over the door from the kitchen to the dining room, a door we pass through dozens of times each day. Our son Dave wrote them in second grade. His childish handwriting is a reminder of how long they have been part of our family life, and how often we rely on their wisdom.

Elsewhere we have posted the Quaker Principles, the Serenity Prayer, the Buddhist Eightfold Path, and Irish, Jewish, and Native American prayers. (Yes, diversity and pluralism prevail in our home.)

Choose a moral compass (or several); then post it where you can see it on a daily basis. Some people wear symbolic jewelry to be reminded of their moral compass. Others display objects around their homes and places of work or set up altars. Whatever serves to remind you, get in the habit of making a conscious effort to think about your moral compass, to let it guide you throughout the day. Most of all, appreciate its wisdom and commit to following its advice. Over the years this small change can strengthen your character and keep your journey in life traveling on the high road.

# Conclusion:
## A Little Pep Talk

If you read this book from cover to cover, have notes lining the margins about all the changes you want to make, and are overwhelmed by the thought of them all, imagine how we are feeling, having written all this advice! We are thinking that we should have started making these small changes decades ago, tempted to start to change each other, tempted to start more than one change at a time. Or tempted to enter a Buddhist monastery.

We may be less than perfect and even less than desirable, after thinking about all the stuff we could be and maybe even should be doing or not-doing. But no, we are *not* going to fall in that trap. No sir-ee, we are not. Not after writing about being your own best friend and smiling and counting your blessings. Instead we are going to "stay with the program," as the cliché goes. (Susan loves clichés, and Larry doesn't always know they are clichés.) We will stay on the path of self-improvement, one small change at a time. Last month Larry stopped talking while he chewed, and Susan stopped chewing ice. Our current change is to restore our standing date. (We actually agreed on something.) Next month Larry is going to work on relationships by not stealing stories, while Susan is going to work on her mind and commit to memorizing a poem by Sherman Alexie about playing basketball on a Native American reservation.

So here is our advice to you. *Improve yourself in a gentle way.* Start by thinking about what you have been reading. Pick one small change. Do something to remind you of that change. Next, make another small change. After that, make still another.

Keep making small changes, and in three years you will have taken dozens of small steps toward self-improvement. In ten years, you will have changed your life. Imagine making small changes, one at a time, for as long as you live—and watch the small changes add up.

# About the Authors

PHOTO BY BRUCE FORD

Susan and Larry Terkel have been happily married since 1970, raised three children, and pursued a wide variety of interests along the way. They are graduates of Cornell University, where Larry earned both a B.S. and an M.B.A. and Susan earned a B.S. in Human Ecology and Family Relationships. Larry also earned an M.A. in Philosophy from Kent State University.

In 1978, the couple purchased the Old Church on the Green in Hudson, Ohio, and founded the Spiritual Life Society, an interdenominational center for holistic studies. Larry is licensed as its minister, teaches yoga, meditation, and philosophy, and has officiated at more than two thousand weddings as well as funerals, baby blessings, and other spiritual occasions. Susan runs the center's cultural activities, which have included art shows, poetry readings, concerts, plays, workshops, and special events.

Susan is the author of fifteen books for children and young adults, which focus on ethical, medical, and social issues. She is also a painter and fiber artist. She sells hand-painted wooden knobs to distributors throughout the United States.

For nearly three decades, Larry served as president of a Midwest manufacturing company. In 1996 he founded Global Health Care, Inc., a distributor of rapid bio-medical diagnostics, with offices in both the United States and Mexico. He remains its president.

Please visit their website at www.smallchange.info